Domestic Abuse, Homicide and

Also by Jane Monckton Smith

INTRODUCING FORENSIC AND CRIMINAL INVESTIGATION (2013)
MURDER, GENDER AND THE MEDIA: Narratives of Dangerous Love (2012)
RELATING RAPE AND MURDER: Narratives of Sex, Death and Gender (2010)

Domestic Abuse, Homicide and Gender

Strategies for Policy and Practice

Jane Monckton Smith
Senior Lecturer in Criminology, University of Gloucestershire, UK

and

Amanda Williams
Senior Paramedic, Welsh Ambulance Services NHS Trust, UK

With

Frank Mullane
Director of AAFDA (Advocacy After Fatal Domestic Abuse)

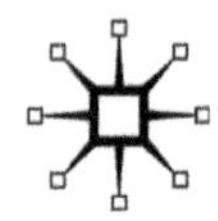

First published 2014 by
PALGRAVE MACMILLAN

Palgrave Macmillan in the UK is an imprint of Macmillan Publishers Limited, registered in England, company number 785998, of Houndmills, Basingstoke, Hampshire RG21 6XS.

Palgrave Macmillan in the US is a division of St Martin's Press LLC, 175 Fifth Avenue, New York, NY 10010.

Palgrave Macmillan is the global academic imprint of the above companies and has companies and representatives throughout the world.

Palgrave® and Macmillan® are registered trademarks in the United States, the United Kingdom, Europe and other countries

ISBN: 978–1–137–30741–5 hardback
978–1–137–30742–2 paperback

This book is printed on paper suitable for recycling and made from fully managed and sustained forest sources. Logging, pulping and manufacturing processes are expected to conform to the environmental regulations of the country of origin.

A catalogue record for this book is available from the British Library.

A catalog record for this book is available from the Library of Congress.

This book is dedicated to the memory of

Eystna Blunnie and of her daughter Rose Louise Blunnie

This book is dedicated to the memory of

Evelin Thomas and of her daughter [illegible]

Contents

Foreword

I am the mother of Samantha who was taken from us on 29 April 2012. Although Samantha was taken in such a cruel and horrific way, I feel no bitterness towards the perpetrator. He took Samantha but he can never take away all the memories that her family had with her. It is coming up to the second birthday without her and although she has roses every week next to her picture and a candle to light her way, no one will know what I would give to have one more minute with her or just to talk to her on the phone; her number is there on my phone. She left three beautiful girls and sisters and a brother, all with memories of her. With this in mind, I hope that Samantha will not be forgotten. I hope in my heart that no other mother or family go through this. You find strength and the ability to carry on for your lost loved one. They have to have a voice as no one else can speak for them; only the ones left behind; we are the ones that can speak for them. They must not be forgotten and all the services must learn from all the mistakes made and admit to the mistakes, no matter how small; the answers mean so much to the loved ones left behind. This is not to apportion blame or point the finger at any one department or service. Just give the answers to the questions that we ask as life is precious and we need as much information as we can get. The curriculum states that every young person should learn English and Maths, we should also be teaching respect and to honour each other. Relationships should be taught from a young age, both at home and in school. Let's make a difference. Either now, or in the future.

Sharon Warren

Acknowledgements

It is important for me to acknowledge the valued assistance provided by Ali Morris (BA, Dip SW, Dip Applied Social Studies), Domestic Abuse and Sexual Violence Coordinator, City and County of Swansea, and Alison Davies, Lead Nurse Mental Health and Safeguarding, Welsh Ambulance Services NHS Trust. Sincere thanks are extended to my sister who, despite enduring significant personal challenges, encouraged me to write down my own personal experiences and to collate and share the thoughts and feelings of EMS colleagues who kindly agreed to participate in supporting this book.

Finally, thanks to my husband Andrew and my family for their ongoing patience

Amanda Williams

I have learned so much researching this book. I still have so much to learn.

Thank you Lina Soper my dear friend for being an angel sent into my life, thank you my sister Amanda, I would not have survived last year without you, thank you Mum and Dad for being patient while I negotiated my illness around you, and thank you my wonderful children Rhiannon, Ffion and Kieran

Jane Monckton Smith

I have been lucky to work with Dr. Jane Monckton Smith who has taken my understanding of domestic abuse to a much higher level. I thank all of the families of homicide victims that I have worked with. They have helped me develop a detailed picture of the gap in status between these families and the state agencies they meet. Thank you to all my family for all of their support, especially my dear mother.

Frank Mullane

About the Authors

Dr Jane Monckton Smith, Jane is Senior Lecturer in Criminology at the University of Gloucestershire. She specialises in homicide and violence, especially domestic homicide, and advises police on a local and national level in domestic abuse and homicide policy. She is the author of *Murder Gender and the Media,* a research study examining the forensic narratives in 72 cases of domestic homicide; *Relating Rape and Murder,* a research study into the relationship between the offences of rape and murder; and *Introducing Forensic and Criminal Investigation,* a guide to complex investigations for students and police recruits. Jane is an Independent Chair for Domestic Homicide Reviews and works for the charity Advocacy After Fatal Domestic Abuse.

Amanda Williams, MCoP Paramedic MA, BA (hons), Amanda joined the Welsh Ambulance Services NHS Trust over 20 years ago and has worked extensively in the pre-hospital emergency arena. As a Practitioner Educator and Safeguarding Tutor, Amanda played a significant role in developing the university curriculum for modern paramedic education in Wales; she is now a Senior Paramedic and NHS Project Manager. She recently completed a three-year research fellowship with the University of Warwick and is an Honorary Lecturer at Swansea University.

Frank Mullane, BSc (hons) DMS ACMA CGMA, Frank is the director of AAFDA (Advocacy After Fatal Domestic Abuse), a charity specialising in helping families after domestic homicide. He lobbied for many years to ensure that Domestic Homicide Reviews became law and helped to develop the statutory guidance underpinning them. He has consistently represented that families, friends and community members should be given the opportunity to be integral to these and other inquiries not just to be involved. He is a member of the national panel that quality assures these reviews and one of a small number of Home Office appointed readers that are asked to assess individual reviews. Frank is a Home Office accredited independent Chair for these inquiries and an advisor to Sequelí (a not for profit social enterprise providing training for Chairs of Domestic Homicide Reviews and other inquiries). He is a visiting university lecturer and student assessor. He previously worked as a business consultant leading teams on change programmes and is a qualified accountant.

1
An Introduction

In March 2014 Her Majesty's Inspectorate of Constabulary (HMIC) published a report into the police response to domestic abuse in England and Wales. They inspected all 43 Home Office funded police services, and concluded that only eight gave a good service to victims. They claimed that domestic abuse was a priority on paper, but not in practice, despite the fact that most police forces and most Police and Crime Commissioners stated it as a priority. HMIC (2014) state that from the evidence collected, domestic abuse is treated as a poor relation to other types of crime. One of the key criticisms was that officers did not have the skills or knowledge necessary to respond to domestic abuse. This was a severe criticism and, given that domestic homicide of women by their intimate partners remains the biggest single female category of homicide, there are serious repercussions for victims.

Sweetnam's (2013) personal account of where domestic abuse hurts is a sobering article and illustrates how abuse and control take over every aspect of the victim. This leaves them with few choices and less room for action. This kind of abuse and control has been variously described as everyday or intimate terrorism (Pain 2013) or compared to hostage taking (Stark 2007). These terms capture how fear is used to maintain control more efficiently than terms like domestic abuse or violence that have very strong associations with overt violence and anger, which seem to be intractable. Victims of everyday terrorism, or IPA, or domestic abuse, whichever terminology is used, are frequently misunderstood by all the agencies they come into contact with. It should be remembered, and HMIC acknowledge this, that it is more than the police response that needs improving. Very often the police take the majority of the criticism for the official response, while other professionals do not have the same expectation placed upon them to deal with domestic abuse effectively, or even appropriately. Health services, for example, may practice what is called Routine Enquiry (RE), and some of them, notably paramedics, may also deal with emergency situations, often with the police. But there is not the same high profile scrutiny of their effectiveness in dealing with domestic abuse. No one is really dealing well with domestic abuse, and much of the blame for this is put on the shoulders of the victims themselves.

Domestic abuse is quite a broad category, but we wish to focus on the biggest type, and one which seems to cause the most frustration among professionals and public, which results in most deaths and life-altering control, and is not only a local problem, but is significant nationally and globally. A second reason for focusing on one category is that different categories of abuse and homicide have different dynamics, motivations and outcomes, so to discuss the problems at a detailed enough level there is a need to focus. Our focus for this research is on women as victims of Intimate Partner Abuse, where the perpetrators were men. Some of the issues are relevant across many categories of abuse, but we just want to make it clear that our suggestions *may* be more relevant to female victims with male abusers, although this is not necessarily always the case. Some problems are the same across different categories. After a session we delivered to police officers and PCSOs on domestic homicide a male officer disclosed to us that he had been the victim of abuse and control by his former wife. This officer was clearly distressed by the memory, and told a story of terrible psychological suffering and hateful bullying. It was a solemn reminder that abuse is widespread, and can be suffered by a diverse number of victim groups. Whilst the motivations of the perpetrators may vary across different types of abuse, the damage to the health and wellbeing of the victim, and to society, is the same. Throughout the book we will refer to domestic abuse, and sometimes more specifically to Intimate Partner Abuse (IPA), domestic homicide and Intimate Partner Femicide (IPF). We will refer to men who abuse as either perpetrators or abusers. We refer to women who are abused, as victims. We cannot, for obvious reasons, use the term survivor, which is often preferred by those victims who did survive. We refer to men and women specifically because we are discussing coercive control and male motivation. However, our recommendations should be a good basic framework for responding to any victim of any kind of abuse.

The most important outcome of this research was to align the victim's perspective as told to us, with the professional perspective, as told to us. We interviewed widely with victims of abuse, and the families of homicide victims, as well as interviewing police officers, paramedics and police support staff. This was achieved through convenience sampling, and was a particularly effective method for us because we come into contact with professionals and victims on a daily basis. For example, we spoke with victims as they presented to us in our professional roles, or they were students of ours, or friends, or patients. Women were keen to talk to us, even those who were currently suffering abuse. Not all our conversations were formal, some were snatched in corridors or ladies toilets, some were more structured and conventional. Similarly, when we spoke with professionals we talked when we could, rather than having a particular formal schedule all the time, though in some cases there were formal focus groups. We found ourselves talking about domestic abuse to a lot of people, because a lot of people come across abuse in their work and their lives. When people know you work in this area they will sometimes disclose their past or present troubles, and it saddens us to say that it is more widespread than we thought. We came across many women abused by their intimate partners, but we also heard stories of men and women abused by their mothers or fathers, and sometimes sons or daughters. Elder abuse is a growing problem (Muller 2014) and many women, as well as men, are involved in this type of abuse. Domestic abuse is about power relationships. It can only be practised when one person has power over another, not only physical power, but possibly financial, emotional, political or structural. This may be a partial explanation for why women are not as well represented as men as intimate partner abusers, they don't have the necessary physical, political or structural power. But we do see domestic abuse perpetrated by women where they do have power over others, as in elder abuse or abuse of children, or other vulnerable family members. Women often have a role in perpetuating and assisting in, so-called, honour violence.

We want to differentiate between domestic arguing, which may or may not include violence, and domestic abuse, which is achieved through control through fear. Domestic arguing is commonplace, and many men and women assault each other without there being ongoing coercive control and abuse. This is the area in which we find most bilateral violence (BV), which is sometimes confused with domestic abuse. It is when the violence is used as a means of control, that it is domestic abuse. We really must differentiate. Domestic arguing and domestic abuse seem to come under the umbrella term of 'domestics' and this is lowering the status of domestic abuse and its seriousness (Pence and Sadusky 2009). We do not suggest that domestic arguing should not be taken seriously, we do suggest the motivations and dynamics are different from abuse through coercive control. Abuse of power happens all the time, but domestic abuse in this context occurs when that abuse becomes controlling and is maintained by fear. This is why the language of everyday terrorism is pertinent (Pain 2014, Sloan-Lynch 2012). We focus on women as victims of intimate partner abuse because it is so widespread; because it reflects the relative inequality in power between male and female roles in a family or relationship; and because of the way certain men use fear either to keep women from leaving them or retaining them as their exclusive sexual or domestic commodity.

In initial interviews with professionals, and to get a feel for the problems and perceptions of domestic abuse and, more specifically for our purposes, of Intimate Partner Abuse (IPA), we asked them to tell us what frustrated them most about responding to domestic abuse. We kept coming across two key complaints: 'Why doesn't she just leave?' and 'Why won't she support a prosecution?' Such was the ubiquity of these complaints that we felt we wanted to address them. In our initial interviews with victims and their families, we asked them how they managed their safety on a day to day basis. Equal amounts of frustration were expressed as in the professional response to IPA. Police were seen as uncaring, as easily manipulated by abusers, and as disbelieving victims. However, the victims were also quite clear on how they managed their safety, and they all had variations of the same basic strategy, that was to demonstrate devotion. This so closely aligns with abuser anxieties about abandonment and rejection that we could see how the power relationship thrived on such an exchange. He demands devotion, she demonstrates it; but it is a dysfunctional need in him, and a dysfunctional fear-driven response by her. No one is thriving in this traumatic exchange. He will feel more and more anxious and paranoid, adding to his problems, and she will become more and more fearful and desperate to leave, though unable to achieve it (Pain 2014, Brown et al. 2010, Websdale 2010, Liem and Roberts 2009, Starzomski and Nussbaum 2000).

Gathering data was an enlightening journey, full of contradiction and complexity, and our work certainly raises many more questions for our communities, our professionals and our legislature about their perceptions of IPA than it could ever answer. It is also true that the subject is much bigger than could be discussed adequately in this text. So we decided to focus very clearly on two areas for data gathering and analysis, and on two issues for discussion in the context of IPA as a specific category of domestic abuse.

First, in respect of talking about frustrations when responding to domestic abuse, we decided to keep this focused on the *point of first contact*. This largely meant we contained our discussions within the context of a 999 call for help from police or paramedics. We felt that, whilst there are other dimensions and different responses further along the line, discussions with professionals of the two questions in this initial response context, were relevant at all stages of the criminal justice process. We have also included a summary of some research, with kind permission of Ali Morris in Chapter 5, which mirrors our own in some respects and had similar findings. So in this respect we sought peer validation. Our second point for data gathering was to speak widely with victims, and the families of deceased victims, to explore safety strategy and how or why they don't always leave abusers immediately, or won't always support prosecutions. We did not simply ask women to answer these two questions, we took the position that the women were more than likely to be using strategies to keep themselves safe which impacted on their decision whether to leave or whether to support a prosecution. So we talked to victims about their strategies to stay safe in order to try and understand what managing a dangerous man is like on a day to day basis. The findings were edifying. They address the two key complaints made by professionals and reveal a disconnection between the victim's perspective and the professional's perspective. We include validating findings for this part of our research in Chapter 8, kindly written and provided by Frank Mullane.

We found that many of the problems and frustrations can be framed within a discussion of status and strategy. So this is how we frame our analysis. This book does not set itself up to provide all the answers for responding to domestic abuse, but it does begin to suggest an alternative model for understanding victims and perpetrators, and makes some tentative recommendations for future practice, which we hope will, at the very least, provoke more research and discussion. More than anything we want to align professional and victim perspectives since the disconnect is dangerous and debilitating for victims. It may exacerbate the problems they experience, and it is certainly not helping to reduce the number of homicides.

This book has been a long journey, bringing together many agendas and perspectives. It is written by a criminologist (with some police experience), and a paramedic (with training experience) and Frank Mullane, who is a professional in the area of domestic homicide and a victim's advocate, as well as being an indirect victim of domestic homicide himself. We were able to have conversations with experts in the area from around the world and are grateful for comments provided by Evan Stark, Neil Websdale and Jacquelyn Campbell. The perspectives in this book are quite wide. It was a dynamic process and the learning was ongoing, and because of this the publishers were presented with quite a different book from that first proposed. We always knew that we wanted the book to be read by professionals, victims, their families, students, academics and any other interested party; quite a broad remit, and we think we have managed to present our findings in a way that is accessible and relevant to all.

Because we have focused clearly on status and strategy, there are many issues we have not discussed. When we talk about a victim's reluctance to disclose abuse we frame our arguments in the language of chronic fear, though we acknowledge there are often more complex barriers in play, including shame, loyalty, gender identity and family unity (Othman et al. 2014). We also acknowledge that we have not openly discussed the differing experiences of women from minority ethnic groups, disabled women, lesbian women, middle class or privileged women, transgender women, older or younger women, and the multitude of quite different groups which may each have a unique perspective. We have tried to talk about gender and the general differences in power and identity between men and women, and the discursive norms that polarise men and women. However, we believe that many of the issues we discuss will be relevant across groups, but are mindful that development of our recommendations may need bespoke tailoring in the future. We have talked about a general and quite universal strategy that women said they used to stay safe and manage their abuse. We have also talked about more status for women as victims in the way they are treated, and the way they are perceived and assessed.

We use Foucault's ideas of discourse as a medium for creating meaning to structure our analysis, whilst at the same time taking a woman-centred view, which draws from the second and third waves of feminism, and celebrates the developing successes of fourth and fifth wave feminism. This book, however, is not heavy with theoretical dialogue, and this is purposeful too. We are bordering on polemicism in places, engaged with organisational agendas in others, deeply concerned with victim experience and strategy in large part, and use a decisively practical focus throughout. We wanted to write the book we had been asked to write by victims and professionals as we completed this journey, a book for victims and professionals to read and draw understanding from. We are clear in our aims: we want to align the victim and professional perspectives to build a better response to domestic abuse calls for help, and to resist the dominant discursive constructions of the abuse, the abused and the abuser.

Structure of the book

We begin this book by discussing status and quite clearly identifying exactly where and how domestic abuse and its victims lose status. We also consider the idea that if the definition for abuse is re-written then of necessity we must re-write the abused and the abuser. Professor Evan Stark's (2013) assertion that we must raise the status of domestic abuse in order to end it, will frame the arguments presented. We seek to try and rebuild our collective idea of both abusers and victims, drawing largely from those women who have been abused, but also from practitioners and professionals involved in delivering services to victims of abuse. Research has suggested that it is the victim who knows the abuser and his practices the best, but who is the least listened to (Monckton Smith 2012). This book, this research, does not seek to build a psychological profile of the abuser, but it will suggest that he is not 'any man' and that there are many psychological and psycho-social models to draw from. Neither does this research seek to build a psychological profile of the victim, but we do talk about chronic fear and the practicalities of living with abuse, how it is managed, and why it is so difficult to leave. We argue that a shift in perceptions of abused and abuser could be the catalyst for forming more effective methods to deal with domestic abuse and raising the status of the abuse and the victim.

We have just presented the framework for the arguments explored in this book. In the following chapters we will develop those ideas drawing on interviews with victims, families and friends of victims (of victims both alive and deceased), professionals, practitioners, and researchers: Chapter 1, this chapter, introduces the context in which this book explores the issue of domestic abuse and defines what we mean by the terms; Chapter 2 is a discussion of status and introduces the idea of Foucauldian discourse, and how the dominant discourse of domestic abuse, or IPA, reduces the status of the abuse and its victims. We describe in detail how status is lost. In Chapter 3 we begin to resist the dominant discourses and contemplate a different discursive approach, framing our discussion around the new definition for domestic abuse; with a consideration of status; Chapter 4 gives an overview of the scale and nature of domestic homicide, who the abusers are, and how victims are responded to; Chapter 5 looks at some current domestic abuse policy and practice, with a particular focus on paramedics in Wales and on police officers more generally; Chapter 6 considers the things said to us by professionals who respond to domestic abuse, specifically police officers, paramedics and support staff. We present a discussion of their frustrations and experiences drawn from interviews and focus groups. In Chapter 7 we present comments made to us by victims of abuse, and by the families of deceased victims. The focus in this chapter is the victim's day to day experiences and how they manage their safety. Chapter 8 is written by Frank Mullane, who talks about the status of the friends and families of domestic homicide victims, that is women who are dead as a result of abuse. Comments about experience, and recommendations for future practice, structure this chapter. Chapter 9 considers everything said to us by many different professionals, victims and victim's families about the frontline response of professionals to domestic abuse. We align the different perspectives and, with a consideration of the extant research, we make some tentative recommendations for future practice. These recommendations construct the victim as rational and justified in the decisions she makes. We resist the idea that she is a problem, and put together suggestions for a *Domestic Abuse Toolkit* for first responders. This toolkit is now available for use by multiple agencies.

In summary, we argue that we need to raise the status of the abuse and of the victim. This position is the catalyst for the arguments which focus on reconstructing our collective understanding of domestic abuse and IPA, in line with the new definition for domestic abuse. It is still the case that many, if not most, social care and criminal justice professionals do not recognise abuse or its victims and perpetrators. There are a huge number of misconceptions and misunderstandings about domestic abuse and its practice, largely perpetuated in dominant discourses (Peters 2008, Stark 2007). Even though the definition has changed, none of the stereotypes or prejudices have been meaningfully challenged in media, criminal justice or culture. If the abuse has been re-written we need to seriously attempt to re-write the actors, at least for our purposes, at the level of criminal justice intervention. Many debates about domestic abuse revolve around the criminal justice response to victims, and the punishment of perpetrators. Whilst there are many other contexts in which to discuss the issues we will for the moment, focus here. We discuss the two key questions and the frustrations caused primarily in a criminal justice context. It is understandable that criminal justice is a focus, for many women end up dead, either by homicide, suicide, neglect, homelessness, substance abuse or illness.

2
Status

How do you get rid of it? Raise the status of it

During a masterclass in understanding Intimate Partner Abuse (IPA) one of the speakers, Professor Evan Stark, said quite simply of IPA, 'How do you get rid of it? Raise the status of it'; simple, yet powerful words. There have been many powerful and persistent voices over the years doggedly trying to raise the status of this abuse. It is certainly the case that they have raised its profile and visibility. They have created services and help for victims. They have overturned some truly awful judicial decisions, they have created expertise, saved lives, protected children, changed policy, held those in authority to account, and raised the profile of women's inequality. Things are changing in the arena of domestic abuse. But the domestic abuse revolution, as Professor Stark puts it, has stalled. Similarly, Dobash and Dobash (2002: 1) state that there has been both 'radical change and no change at all'. The problem seems to lie, as Professor Stark notes, in its status. Even though big changes in policy, process and support have happened, there has been no great change in the way we perceive the abuse or the victims. The implication of this is that the way we actually think about IPA is the real barrier to progress.

We are persuaded by the concept of discourse, as articulated by French philosopher Michel Foucault (1972), when we start to consider how we think about IPA and IPF. To put it simplistically, Foucault argued that everything fits into a social, rather than a natural, category (Thorp 1992). The way we 'know' about everything is within discourses, and discourse is a constructed version of reality rather than a true representation of it. So, from this perspective, the discourse of domestic abuse represents our dominant collective belief at this time about the reality of IPA. There are many different discourses in circulation at any point in time, but some are more dominant than others, and some dominate. It would be instructive then to look at the most dominant discourse of domestic abuse, and explore its impact on the status of IPA and its victims. The problem of domestic abuse and violence against women is highly visible and there is global agreement that it needs to be tackled. So the status of the *problem* is not at issue as much as the status of the practices of abuse, and the status of the primary and indirect victims. Therefore the first task of this research was to begin to identify the truths of this dominant discourse, and then to explore how those truths diminish the status of domestic abuse, or IPA, and its victims. The first step in discourse analysis is to get to know your data (Carabine 2001). We did this in a number of ways: we looked at criminal justice and forensic narratives as a rationalisation for domestic homicide and asked how these narratives can explain what happened and whose fault it was; we also looked at media reporting of domestic homicide to examine journalists's narratives; we looked at feminist and anti-feminist literature; we spoke widely with victims, practitioners and experts. We buried ourselves in the discourse. Quite by chance we came across a small opinion piece in the *Birmingham Mail* which summed up the dominant discourse very effectively, albeit in extreme terms. The author, Maureen Messent, succinctly put the blame for murdered women squarely on their own shoulders for failing to leave their abuser. She said:

> Battered women are Britain's holy cows, never to be held accountable for staying with brutal men, never to be told the harm done to children who watch these beatings...Now we've had an inevitable guest appearance of Her Majesty's Inspectorate of Constabulary (in sackcloth and ashes) to apologise that our police forces are failing to protect women from their assailants. This is less than fair. The women who allow themselves to be used as punch bags are often their own worst enemies. The death toll of domestic violence...is shocking for its avoidability and we're never told how many of the dead refused police advice to leave their attackers once and for all. (Messent 2014)

Such words are the dominant discourse and an excellent illustration of the beliefs that make it possible for abusers to do what they do. The victim is constructed as the problem, the abuser is invisible and barely culpable. When the families and children of deceased victims hear such opinions, they can respond with a very different story. A story of chronic fear and death threats, desperate attempts to leave, repeated calls for help, stalking, violence, bullying, obsession and terror; a terror that experts in the field describe as both rational and justified (Pain 2013). The status of homicide victims in such opinion is so low they appear not to have regard for their own lives, or the lives of their children.

We found that Professor Stark is absolutely right, status is a considerable issue, and in this chapter we begin to deconstruct the discourse, to explore some ways in which status is lost through discursive truths and powerful discursive formations. We discuss the status of the abuse itself first, and then that of the abuse victims. Our frame is first responder professional responses to abuse and its victims. We found that this is where many of the problems with responding to domestic abuse or IPA are being articulated. As noted, the recent HMIC (2014) report into police responses to domestic abuse reflects many of the stated problems with status. So, given that the official definition for domestic abuse has been modified, is apparently to be used to send a new message to abusers and that there is significant dissatisfaction with professional responses, this is where we will focus our attention.

The status of the abuse

The status of domestic abuse as a crime

In the UK the official definition for domestic abuse has been refined to better reflect what we know from research and evidence about it and the way it is practised. The new definition follows a cross government agreement that the age range for victims needed expanding, and that the exertion of coercive control is a crucial element in its practice. This is not new knowledge, control through fear has been acknowledged as a key characteristic of abuse for years. In 1993 the Duluth wheel of power and control effectively showed how abuse works (Pence and Paymar 1993) and second wave feminism had been resisting powerful discourses of abuse since the 1970s. It is merely newly included in the definition. Nick Clegg announced that this new definition would raise the profile of domestic abuse and send the message to perpetrators that their behaviour won't be tolerated (https://www.gov.uk/government/news/new-definition-of-domestic-violence-and-abuse-to-include-16-and-17-year-olds). However, since there has been no corresponding legislation to outlaw the newly included practices of coercion and control and give them any legal status, it remains difficult for criminal justice agencies to respond to domestic abuse or, more specifically for our purposes, IPA. It remains a course of conduct that, if identified, can only be considered in a risk assessment interview as raising the risk level for that particular victim.

This may lead to a referral for support from a specialist agency, but it cannot be responded to as an offence, and this may mean that perpetrator behaviour is left unaddressed. It is not even that coercion and control are not dangerous behaviours which don't require societal attention, or are low status misdemeanours – coercive control and verbal threats are more positively correlated with homicide than violence alone, and should be taken very seriously (Liem and Roberts 2009, Stark 2007). Many argue that using the criminal justice system as the only, or main, response to IPA is neither appropriate nor effective (Hester 2013b, Walklate 2008, Smart 1989) and this is true on multiple levels. Government cannot just walk away from this conundrum without discussing the structures needed to address this problem. If IPA is not to be considered illegal, then the predominant political criminal justice response to domestic abuse is not fit for purpose. Police officers are only able to respond with the tools for crisis management. Domestic abuse is ongoing and resilient to crisis management intervention, so there needs to be a more robust statement of how the new definition will translate into current practice for responding to victims. There is a political focus on prosecution as a deterrent and a means for dealing with domestic abuse, but there is still a reluctance to fully embrace the idea that abuse of an intimate partner is a serious matter. The dominant discursive truth is that domestic abuse is part of 'the cut and thrust of life' (see Chapter 6) and adults should be capable of sorting it out between themselves without outside intervention, except in extreme circumstances. Stark (2013) states that aggressive prosecution should be used in domestic abuse, and that outcomes are better for women who support prosecutions than for those who do not. It is also the case that many more prosecutions would be brought if officers made more use of the current offences available. For example, threats to kill and witness intimidation could be used more effectively. However, evidence for these offences is not being routinely collected, and even the evidence for more traditional charges of assault is not being collected where it exists (HMIC 2014). In this respect there is an argument that we do not need more legislation, we just need to use the legislation we have to better effect. This may be true, but it does not address the issue of status. Domestic abuse is discursively considered a private matter in which the victim could, in fact, sort out her own problems if she would just leave, and not one for the attention or resources of law enforcement. Giving the practice illegal status may go some way to resisting this myth.

The Government gesture which changes the definition, which explicitly acknowledges the research and experience, is a win in the domestic abuse revolution. The floodgates have officially opened for a debate about change. There are, of course, complex issues in writing domestic abuse, as a course of conduct, into black letter law. Victims may well end up being treated as perpetrators if the practices of coercive control are not carefully articulated and understood. The status of the victim may be a significant bar to a response which is always in the spirit of any new legislation. A victim's 'course of conduct' in response to domestic abuse is often easily manipulated to appear that they are the problem. It is already a problem that police are more willing to arrest a woman in a domestic abuse call, and that women are three times more likely to be arrested (Hester 2013b). It is not only victims who are manipulated by abusers, police are too. There are dangers inherent in trying to articulate a deeply hidden course of conduct into a visible criminal pattern. However, the, so-called, *Stalking Act* set a precedent for writing courses of conduct into law. The amendments to the *Protection from Harassment Act 1997*, which were made through the *Protection of Freedoms Act 2012*, outlawed, so-called, stalking behaviour. Stalking is not specifically defined, but courses of conduct which constitute harassment can be considered stalking, and there are *example* behaviours listed (National Stalking Helpline 2014).

There are discussions and consultations happening at government level as we write this which specifically address whether to name domestic abuse as a crime. It is true that at this time there is legislation which exists to respond to *some* of the violence which characterises domestic abuse, as we have just discussed. Certainly, we have laws against rape, stalking, GBH, ABH, common assault, breach of the peace, witness intimidation and threats to kill; crimes which can dominate the experience of domestic abuse victims. However, the insidious methods of threat and control, which more accurately characterise the abuse, are not included in this legislation. Domestic abuse is a pattern of behaviour or course of conduct characterised by actions which, at their most sinister and dangerous, do not necessarily always infract the criminal law. The practice of coercive control is not made up of discrete incidents of abuse or violence (Hester 2013b, Stark 2007). It really is not the point that there are named crimes which *can* address *some* of the behaviours which *can* characterise domestic abuse. The fact is, in terms of status, the practice itself is not yet declared illegal, nor is there a clear pathway for the emergency services to deal with it. The problem of domestic abuse is popularly believed to be owned by the police (Hester 2013b) and our research suggests that other services perceive it as a criminal justice problem, though the police feel it is more of a social than a crime issue (see Chapter 6). The problem of domestic abuse appears to have no willing owner and this could be because there is no clear alignment with any particular organisational agenda. The police struggle to respond to domestic abuse, and they are not adequately equipped to respond to coercion and control.

Status is bestowed by Acts of Parliament. Domestic abuse could be acknowledged as wholly unacceptable by making it and its practice explicitly illegal, and/or making sure that it is easily recognised and identified with a clear pathway for a response. Criminal sanction is just one response. Many abusers are dysfunctional on many levels and there may be appropriate health, mental health, or substance abuse and anger management interventions. These kinds of intervention may need powers and legislation attached to make sure of abuser compliance. There are many ways that more status could be given officially to send the message that abuse is unacceptable.

As we have noted, it is acknowledged that IPA should not be considered as individual, isolated violent assaults with a proximal cause, but as an ongoing *pattern* of behaviour, which is controlling and threatening. The concept of control is more consistent in cases of abuse, than is violence (Websdale 2010, Stark 2007, Adams 2007). Violence may be used to achieve control, but there are many more methods and practices to achieve it. As has been noted in previous research, in some cases the mere threat of violence is enough (Stark 2007, Felder and Victor 1997), especially if it has been used to powerful effect in the past. However, in our current legal system, and indeed in our cultural belief systems, abuse without violence is difficult to respond to. It is not against the law to exert control, it does not have the status of a crime. What we do know is that certain men who need to control their partners, or feel a diminishing sense of control in their lives, can become very dangerous (Websdale 2010, Adams 2007, Stark 2007). There have been great strides made in accepting that abuse can be more than violence, and that violence is more than beating, but whilst some of the less explicitly violent practices are recognised, there is little understanding of the gravity of what can occur when a man is controlling and abusive. It has long been acknowledged that there are domestic abuse myths, that is 'truths' constructed within the dominant discourse of domestic abuse (Peters 2008). This dominant discourse is a powerful prism which bends how we understand what abuse is and how it is practised. Unfortunately, it is not only that 'members of the public' have their judgement swayed by the myths, many professionals and policymakers also draw from this belief system when responding to IPA. This may mean that we are not implementing the best policies, or that good policies are being poorly implemented. Importantly, it also influences those who are performing risk assessments. Some very dangerous behaviours are not recognised or treated seriously, and victims are then not given the priority or support they require. Many of the homicides we come across were risk assessed at medium or standard levels, some were not seen as serious enough to warrant a risk assessment at all. Yet in every case coercion and control were present.

We accept that writing domestic abuse into law may be too complex to benefit victims because of its, and their, lack of status. But half a criminal justice response is insufficient and potentially dangerous. If government acknowledge that domestic abuse is practised in a certain way, and that that is unacceptable, then they must consider the official response. Outside of crisis management by emergency services, it is organisations with charitable status that routinely respond to and manage ongoing IPA. These charities are largely underfunded and struggle to give the level of service they would like. Their work often involves managing the safety of victims whose lives have been threatened. It is not their task to deal with perpetrators, though they are increasingly considering and offering perpetrator programmes. It is testament to the low status of IPA that the police do not even want ownership of this behaviour by some of the most dangerous people in our communities, which often leads to criminal assault and homicide,

Domestic Abuse Case Study 1: Elliot Turner

Elliot Turner murdered 17-year-old Emily Longley on 7 May 2011 by strangling her at his Bournemouth home where he lived with his parents. Turner told police he didn't know how she had died. His parents destroyed evidence and lied to the police to protect their son and were both jailed for conspiracy to pervert the course of justice. Turner was found guilty of murder and sentenced to life with a tariff of sixteen years. He was a man described as having a narcissistic personality disorder. His abuse of Emily was known and documented. He was so convinced of the rightness of his perspective, and that he had the support of friends he had told that he planned to kill her, and who even allowed him to practice strangling them in preparation. He frightened her, he threatened her and he stalked her. No one took him seriously because it was 'domestic'. All the high risk signs that Emily was in serious danger were present, but no one considered that she needed help, or that Turner needed reporting to the police. This kind of domestic abuse, especially of very young girls, is not taken seriously. His parents even colluded with him to hide the murder of this young, vulnerable and intimidated girl. The police caught them discussing destroying evidence by using covert means.

The status of the practices of abuse

The status of coercive control and domestic abuse at this macro level is not high enough. But there are problems of status at the micro level too. The violence model which dominates the understanding of domestic abuse and which is part of the dominant discourse operates at the micro level.

The violence model

The violence model characterises abuse as made up of isolated incidents of violence with some proximal cause, and enjoys the highest status in terms of what we consider abuse. It is the case that our criminal justice response is geared up to respond to this model, which is: there is a moment of crisis and violence, the police attend, deal with the immediate crisis and the violence, and then leave. But it has been long known that the violence model is often inadequate, inappropriate, dangerous and demonstrably ineffective. The violence model seems to better characterise a domestic argument, rather than domestic abuse. Whilst a domestic argument can be serious and have devastating outcomes, it is not the same as ongoing control and abuse. Pence and Sadusky (2009) articulate the view that context is important, and context will identify control. There are practical reasons, which will be discussed later (see Chapter 4), that can make the violence model response dangerous in a domestic abuse case. But for the moment we will focus on issues of status. If a woman is beaten to a certain standard of injury, as in the violence model, the abuse has more status. By this we mean that a punch to the head which breaks the woman's jaw or cheek will be given far more status by the authorities than low level bullying and physical assault, which creates terror and chronic fear, and is constant and debilitating (Pain 2014). Often, victims who are subject to such constant threat and terror in their lives cannot easily access help. They may resort to substance abuse, which further reduces their status as victims, we have seen many cases where substance abuse has been forced on a victim by an abuser; they may make repeated calls to the police for intervention in what appears to be low level domestic arguing; *she* is then seen as a burden on police resources and a time waster, which reduces her status even further. What she really needs is a broken nose to raise her status as a victim of something the police can actually respond to. In fact, the most vulnerable and seriously abused victims are the ones who are often given the least time and attention across services (Stark 2013, Hester 2013a).

Coercive control is a course of conduct practised over time. It is what Marianne Hester (2013a) describes as a long thin offence. The perpetrators will not always be standing at the door with a woman's blood on their fist ready to be arrested. The abused woman will not always be crying in the street nursing her broken nose and finally ready to support a prosecution. This is the dominant discourse constructing stereotypical subjects to serve the violence model, and reactive policing which uses punishment as its remedy. It is a strong and resilient discourse of abuse which acts to reduce the status of other practices of abuse. We must challenge the stereotypes if we are to respond appropriately to what is now acknowledged in the official definition for domestic abuse, the practice of coercion and control. If we rewrite the practice we must, of necessity, rewrite the perpetrator and victim. Pain (2014) uses the language of everyday terrorism to describe domestic abuse, it is a resistance to dominant discursive truths and eloquently tells of the constant chronic fear and dread suffered by its victims. Websdale uses the language of haunting to explore perpetrator motives in familicide (Websdale 2010). This change in semantics changes how we perceive the problem. These counter discourses do not have the dominance they could, the language of overt violence dominates conversation and imagery in domestic abuse.

In summary, we have discussed two methods by which the *practice of domestic abuse* loses status, at a macro and micro level through discursive practices, and they are:

1. It is not given the status of criminal behaviour
2. The dominant and most dangerous characteristics are downgraded in favour of certain types of physical assault

The status of the woman as victim

In the UK, as in most jurisdictions, we have two competing models for understanding abuse and violence against women. There is the (global) VAWG framework, which explicitly focuses on the contexts and abuses suffered by women because they are women. In the UK there is also the official definition for domestic abuse which frames the problem as *gender neutral*. It is important, in terms of the woman's status as victim, that we discuss issues of gender first.

The level of violence suffered by men the world over is appalling. Homicide against men is not given the publicity or resources it deserves. But it should be remembered that women do not pose much of a risk to men, either in terms of morbidity or mortality. It is other men who pose the biggest safety risk to men. It would be inaccurate to argue that men do not suffer domestic abuse, or that men are not assaulted by women, or that women do not kill men; they do. However, it is shown in research over and again that it is women who suffer the most serious and prolonged campaigns of violence and abuse (Hester 2013a, Stark 2007, Adams 2007, Websdale 1999). Violence against men by their intimate partners is often confined to isolated incidents which do not cause serious injury and, whilst bullying and abuse do cause trauma, isolation and distress for some men, they do not, in general terms, report the same levels of fear. Hester (2013a) suggests that men do not report the fear that women do, nor do they suffer the same kind of injury, or repeated attacks. Whereas women do report fear, they do suffer more serious injury, and they do suffer repeated assaults. Studies show that the predominant motive for women who kill their intimate partners is to protect themselves or their children (Liem and Roberts 2009). There simply aren't the same numbers of men being systematically beaten, abused and controlled. It is also the case that women and men use violence for different reasons. Stark reports higher levels of serious outcomes where bilateral violence (BV) is recorded (Stark 2007). However, Stewart et al. (2012) state that BV is more of a problem than at first thought and is considered less serious and note that in BV it is women who suffer the overwhelming burden of morbidity and mortality. They also note, importantly, that common couple or BV violence can only be considered as such where there is no pattern of control by the male, so this discounts the vast majority of abusive relationships. This is often not factored into arguments which seek to undermine the fact that women are predominantly the victims. Stewart et al. (2012) also comment that when assaulted, male victims report having things thrown at them, being bitten or kicked, hit or slapped; whilst women report being beaten, sexually assaulted, choked, threatened with gun or knife, and having gun or knife used on them.

There is no easy comparison between male and female use of violence in a domestic context. Generally, men use domestic abuse as a life strategy to maintain control, while women, it is argued, use abuse (where it is unrelated to abuse being used on them), to achieve specific short-term goals. What we know is that female and male use of violence and abuse is different, cannot be easily compared, and has different repercussions and outcomes. The biggest problem, universally acknowledged and evidence based, is that women are the group who are most often the victims of serious, long term, life challenging domestic abuse (Hester 2013a, Stark 2013, 2007, Websdale 1999). People in same sex couples, heterosexual and gay men, and transsexuals also suffer abuse and violence; there is no group free from its threat, but Stewart et al. (2012) note that domestic abuse levels appear to be higher in heterosexual couples. However, when we look at the problem nationally, internationally and globally it is overwhelmingly women who are the predominant group suffering homicide, violence, and life altering control. Even if it were the case, which it is not, that men were suffering equal seriousness of abuse at the hands of women, and dying in similar numbers, it would not reduce the problem of violence against women. It would still be the problem it currently is. In fact, the highest risk factor by far in domestic homicide and everyday terrorism, is being female.

Losing status through anti female/feminist rhetoric

Women as victims already suffer from low status because of their gender, and this can be exacerbated by arguments with an anti-female/anti-feminist bias. This bias is often used to undermine the VAWG approach and, in many ways, seeks to reduce the status of women as victims of abuse. Van Wormer and Roberts (2008) states that anti-feminist rhetoric is destructive enough for it to be considered in all discussions of violence against women. Certainly, whenever we have to speak about domestic homicide against women, we have to factor in time to defend our focus on women as victims. It is also our experience that the arguments which assert that women are the predominant victims are often automatically labelled as coming from a particular feminist perspective. Feminism is powerfully framed in popular and news media as a particular perspective that is not the perspective of 'ordinary' people. It is rarely assumed that a person on the street would hold what is represented as a feminist view. But when we speak with students, for example, there is universal agreement that domestic abuse should end and that we need to reduce homicide of women. It is simultaneously a feminist *and* a human view of the world. But feminist arguments are often considered biased, political and anti-men, which is, of course, inaccurate and can leave the veracity of the arguments open to question. This has an effect of reducing the status of *the argument.* It would be naïve to consider that the problems facing women are the same problems facing men. It would also be plain wrong to consider that there isn't a significant and global problem with male violence against women. *There simply is no global epidemic of female violence against men.* The problems faced by women who are abused by men, specifically their intimate partners, are at the very least different, have specific social dynamics and supports, and are experienced and meted out differently. The dominant discourse of feminism and feminists, which constructs them as politically subjective, reduces the status of the arguments.

There is a backlash against the feminist position articulated through discourses of neutrality and equality, which are part of a larger discourse around human rights. Legislation has required that people are treated equally irrespective of gender, for example, and many of the arguments which seek to undermine the focus on women in the context of IPA, refer to the fact that men suffer domestic abuse too. The language of equality and neutrality in this particular anti-feminist context implies that women abuse as much as men, and are as dangerous; that there is equal violence (Flood 2009, Kimmel 2008). This position, as we have discussed, is not validated by experience or research (Flood 2009, Kimmel 2008). It is further argued by some that the terms domestic abuse and intimate partner abuse are too neutral and do not acknowledge the enormous disparity in who is abused and how (Sloan-Lynch 2012). Also, the language of neutrality has permeated the police response (which we discuss further in Chapter 6).Police have reported to us that they see impartiality in domestic abuse calls as necessary, in part to remain neutral. We will argue later that this is a dangerous stance, and one that is not taken when responding to most other crime. There is a cultural distrust of women, which has religious and cultural roots, and permeates the ways in which we respond to all sorts of violence predominantly committed against women, like rape and sexual assault (Kelly et al. 2005, Lees 1997, Brownmiller 1995). These discourses have justified and excused violence against women over the centuries but still have a powerful presence in the cultural psyche. Resisting these discourses is arguably the key to raising the status of women as victims, and the status of domestic abuse. Feminism has been the only real challenge or resistance to these powerful discourses, and is often represented as dishonest (Monckton Smith 2010, Van Wormer 2008). There are a number of men's interest groups that are explicitly anti-feminist and aggressively attack the feminist discourse (Flood 2009). Overwhelming evidence that supports what is represented as a feminist perspective, has not been fully embraced on a cultural level, though we see increasing political and policy interventions which validate this position, and have driven the substantial changes in responding to domestic abuse.

Losing status in the hierarchy of female victims

As we have discussed, types of abuse and violence exist in a hierarchy, and physical violence which causes injury sits at the top. Victims also exist in a hierarchy. If we consider homicide, and female victims of male violence only, the relative status of different categories of female victim are quite visible. At the top of the victim hierarchy is the woman who was killed by a stranger, the woman victim gets lower and lower down the hierarchy the more intimate she is with her killer (Monckton Smith 2010, 2012, Kelly et al. 2005, Cammiss 2006, Dawson 2003, Lees 1997). So, being married to and co-habiting with the killer gives the woman the least status, in both cultural and criminal justice terms. This applies also to abuse and assault (Cammiss 2006, Dawson 2003) and to rape (Kelly et al. 2005), so domestic abuse has the lowest status, even in the context of violence against only women.

If we continue down this hierarchy of female victims, and include the violence model and the way it diminishes the status of the most insidious and dangerous forms of abuse, we can see how the victim of domestic abuse can easily become the subject of frustration and contempt. A woman who suffers *low level* assaults from her *live-in husband* has very low status. She may further lose status if she fails to respond to criminal justice and other interventions in a way which fits with the agenda of a particular organisation. For example, when a woman refuses to support a prosecution, or withdraws her complaint, police officers and lawyers can become frustrated and will often feel there is nothing they can do to help. This can reduce the enthusiasm with which they approach repeated calls for help from that victim. *She* becomes the problem, *she* can be seen as a time waster, as mentally ill, as a drunk. This victim then loses nearly all status, and may be isolated from any of the help available (Hester 2013a).

Of course, there are other factors which have an influence on the status of the woman and which are extra to the problems just mentioned. For example, a woman can further lose status as a result of her ethnicity and her social class. Social class has an impact on domestic abuse from both ends of the spectrum. Middle and upper class women may be even more reluctant to disclose abuse than others. Quite often the abusers are more powerful and have major financial and social control. There is also much to lose in terms of social status. The high profile abuse of Nigella Lawson by her then husband is a good example of this. Women from lower socio-economic groups, who may be unemployed and poorly educated, lose status because of their class. In Chapter 6 police officers discuss the problems caused for them by arguments between people on Facebook, they see this as a, largely lower class, contemptible problem. Women from ethnic minority groups are disproportionately affected by domestic abuse and homicide. Bureau of Justice statistics for 2005 show that African Americans constituted 12.7 per cent of the population, but 24 per cent of spousal homicide victims were African American (cited in Chanmugam 2014). Sullivan and Websdale (2006) state that white women is the only category of domestic homicide which has not fallen. Worldwide, gender is the most significant predictor for domestic abuse and homicide, irrespective of social class or ethnicity.

Losing status through resistance

Another way in which a woman can lose status is by being perceived as weak or reckless. For example, women who do not leave abusive men are often perceived this way. The question 'Why doesn't she leave?' is addressed later in this book. Women who don't leave are seen as causing their own problems and creating problems for everyone else. Clearly, there is a dangerous gap in understanding between the reality of her situation and the perception of it, and an assumption that she even has the choice whether to leave or not. Also, she is criticised for failing to support prosecutions. Hester (2013a) states that abuse victims are using the criminal justice system to manage violence and abuse, not to achieve convictions. So, here again, she loses status and consolidates her position as 'the problem'. At no point in this economy of status exchange is the man or the police officer bartering for their life. The abuser is free to behave very differently, with more confidence, less fear and more societal and cultural solidarity with his position. Research has found that women are refusing even to disclose abuse to health professionals because they are terrified they will be made to leave the abuser or support a prosecution (Orthman et al. 2014). Such is their fear women keep the abuse a secret, yet it is perceived as a stupid, ill-informed decision, rather than the rational and justified decision that it is (Pain 2014).

Losing status through death

When a woman is killed by her intimate partner her status is arguably at its lowest. The criminal justice response focuses significantly on the killer and his narrative of events (Monckton Smith 2012, Lees 1997). This is true in inquests and trials. It is also true of media responses to a domestic homicide. The victim's story is routinely overlooked and ignored. The forensic narrative produced by the police for a prosecution fits an institutional agenda to achieve a conviction and is not necessarily a *search for the truth* (Monckton Smith et al. 2013), the killer's narrative dominates as the system responds to his defences and appeals, and it also dominates in the media. His partial narrative, which is not often robustly challenged, especially if there is a guilty plea, can then stand as the official narrative of events and inform future practice (Monckton Smith 2012, Lees 1997). The victim's story of coercion, control and chronic fear is not told, and so the knowledge we have of the reality of abuse is not shared. Even the victim's family and friends have little opportunity to address the things said about their beloved relative or friend in these narratives. The deceased victim then has little or no voice, which must be the lowest status she has ever endured.

One way in which this is being balanced somewhat is with the introduction of Domestic Homicide Reviews from Section 9 of the *Domestic Violence, Crime and Victims Act (2004)* and which became statutory on 13 April 2011. In these reviews the antecedent history to a domestic homicide is reviewed to learn and implement lessons to try and reduce deaths. In these reviews the victim's story is often finally revealed and told, sometimes for the first time. Families and friends of the victim are also invited to participate in these reviews, which is a clear way of giving some status to the importance of her and their story.

In summary, we have discussed five ways that *women as victims of domestic abuse* lose status in discourses of domestic abuse:

1. Through anti-female and anti-feminist bias
2. Through the intimate relationship with the abuser
3. By being victims of coercive control and not being routinely physically beaten
4. By failing to support the criminal justice agenda and well-meaning advice to leave the relationship
5. When they are killed as a result of domestic abuse and silenced by the system

Domestic Abuse Case Study 2: OJ Simpson

OJ Simpson was accused of killing his former wife, Nicole Brown Simpson, and her friend Ronald Goldman in 1994. Simpson had a documented history of beating Nicole and she told police she was terrified of him and that she was sure he was going to kill her. However, when this case went to trial Simpson was able to deflect the abuse claims and claim instead that Nicole was the batterer, and that the police had only charged him because they were racists. Simpson was found not guilty. He went on to write a book called *If I Did It* telling how he would have killed Nicole and Ronald if it had been him. He was later found liable for their wrongful killings at a civil hearing in 1996 brought by the victims' families. Simpson's celebrity status and claims of racism garnered much solidarity for him and the case is said to have split America along racial lines. The domestic abuse and high risk behaviours were hidden in a wider debate, and Nicole's life experience with Simpson was effectively silenced.

The lack of status afforded to the practice of domestic abuse, and its victims, both direct and indirect, is one of the biggest challenges to ending it. In Chapter 8 Frank Mullane discusses how status affects the families of victims of domestic abuse and homicide in a myriad of ways. Families are often absent in discussions of domestic abuse yet they are frequently at the centre of it, especially after the death of a victim. They may witness the abuse of their daughter or mother or sister, for example, they may watch her being systematically isolated from their care and influence, they may suffer bereavement through homicide, they may be involved in inquests and trials, they may find themselves caring for the children of their deceased loved one. Families are treated badly because victims have low status. Throughout this book we challenge and resist the dominant ways of thinking about domestic abuse, its victims, and its perpetrators. We turn domestic abuse on its head, and Chapters 7 and 8 give voice to a group of victims who have to fight every step of the way to be heard. That is just one reason why it is so important that you read them.

3
Status: New Definition, New Thinking

The new definition

We must acknowledge that if the characteristics of something change then, of necessity, so do the actors. So, when the definition for abuse is changed this changes who the perpetrators and victims are. The new definition, in many ways, resists the dominant discourse of IPA. It should produce new discursive subjects, the most important of whom will be the victim and the abuser. For example, if we say that the definition for GBH requires that the victim receives a broken bone, then all other assaults which do not break bones are excluded and the characteristics of GBH are different. It may also be that people who use the type of violence that breaks bones have different motivations and psychology from those who cause serious injury by, for example, throwing acid. This will mean that the people who commit GBH and those who are its victims are changed also. Previous perceptions and constructions of GBH victims and perpetrators are no longer wholly valid. Foucault's (1972) idea that we construct our own reality through discourse has an immediate relevance. Now that it has been acknowledged specifically that domestic abuse is a course of conduct that involves coercion and control, new discursive subjects are constructed. Now we have to know about those abusers who are not merely physically violent, but are controlling and have a different psychology, and we must also consider those victims whose lives are dominated by fear rather than injury. These are different people and different subjects from the stereotypical actors in the dominant discourse of IPA and the violence model it has constructed. I do not suggest that this knowledge of domestic abuse and its practice is new. It is merely newly *included* in the definition. In this respect we can perhaps see where the *disconnect* liesbetween current attitudes and beliefs about IPA and reality. There is a new language and discursive position developing, the language of *everyday* or *intimate terrorism* (Pain 2013, 2014), and this discourse draws a parallel between domestic abuse and terrorism, in the context that they both use fear to exert control. It is possible to resist discursive knowledge, and the counter discourses of everyday terrorism for example are evidence of that resistance. Allen (2003) discusses how young people negotiate their sexual identities through discursive resistance to dominant discourses of heterosexuality, and don't just passively receive the 'truths' of sexuality that it promulgates. The dominant discourse of IPA is very closely related to discourses of heterosexuality and heteronormativity. These powerful discourses construct what is 'normal' and, whilst there is room for resistance, sometimes sexual and gender identity has a unique power to make individuals especially vulnerable. Pain discusses how gender inequality is a significant factor in domestic abuse as its effects reflect the social and political structures that reinforce it (2013: 8). Lees (1997) showed this to great effect when she looked at young women trying to avoid being labelled a 'slag'. Even whilst these women and girls resisted the discursive knowledge about slags, they didn't want to be so labelled. Most people agree that domestic abuse is a terrible and dangerous practice, and on an intuitive level most people recognise that women are especially vulnerable. However, discourses of heterosexuality and romantic love, which tell us what is normal in gender performance in intimate relationships, tell us that men are violent and controlling as a natural output of their biology. This creates a dilemma which adds to the complexities, for the abusers and victims do not sit outside the discourse. Women will often tolerate terrible abuse because they think it's normal, and men will justify their own abuse with reference to their biology. But further than this, many problems have been identified in abusers which relate to the specific pressures and expectations put on them as a result of their gender (Websdale 2010, Brown et al. 2010). Men are as constrained by their gender identity as women, and female tolerance of some abuse, is as discursively produced as some of the causes of that abuse. Resistance to the dominant discourse is crucial in addressing these particular issues.

Police officers and other professionals have been given the tools to respond to the violence model, the simplistic psychology it suggests, and the straightforward criminal justice response it relies on. This might suggest that those in power consider that the violence model *is* the problem of IPA, this gives it some status as the truth. But female deaths at the hands of abusers have remained fairly static, and calls for help against domestic abuse are rising according to Yvette Cooper, the current shadow Home Secretary (2013). The model is not appropriate and the response is not fit for purpose. If the aim of the criminal justice response is to keep people safe and reduce IPA and IPF, it is not working.

The IPA myths which dominate the criminal justice response (Peters 2008) suggest that women who are abused are weak or reckless and are suffering not only from violent assaults, but also from what is referred to as psychological abuse. Psychological abuse is very often simplistically constructed as insults which diminish the confidence of the woman. We would suggest that we need to rethink all of these aspects to abuse – what violence is, what psychological abuse is, and what we think of as 'weak'. Similarly, the abuser is not one dimensional and we have many misunderstandings about him. The myths construct him as a violent bully whose violence gets progressively worse (Peters 2008). It constructs him as responding to some trigger which makes him get angry, lose his temper and start beating the victim. It paints the picture of someone 'losing control' and this language is routinely used to explain the violence used in domestic homicides (Monckton Smith 2012, Stark 2007). This construction does not match with the profile of all, or even most, of the men who commit abuse. It is far more useful to appreciate his behaviour as EXERTING control, rather than losing it (Stark 2009). Abusers are very often obsessive and dependent men who are acting out of fear of losing control of the woman and thus, as they see it, of their lives (Brown et al. 2010, Websdale 2010). Sometimes circumstances will diminish the amount of control these men have over their lives through, for example, financial crises (Websdale 2010). Sometimes it is a deep seated fear of losing the woman, but coupled with a sense of entitlement and ownership which is often tacitly supported in cultural and societal beliefs, structures and practices (Stark 2007).

Nancy Berns (2004) argues that the way a social problem is constructed or presented, can suggest the solution to that problem. For example Cohen (2002) gives us the example of groups of young men acting together in a way which causes concern or fear. If the young men are perceived as criminal and violent, this suggests a criminal justice or police intervention; however, if the young men are perceived as bored and disaffected then the solution may be to provide them with more leisure facilities. The way the problem and the actors are framed can suggest the solution to the problem. In this respect the discourse which is providing ourknowledgeof the problem will be central in responding to the problem. So, using this framework, if we perceive domestic abuse perpetrators as one dimensionally violent, the logical solution may seem to be to punish that violence until it stops; a very paternalistic response. However, if the perpetrator is perceived as dependent, dangerously manipulative and obsessive, then our solution may be different. This is a different discourse for IPA. It tells us of the *ongoing* danger to the victim, and does not fit with the violence model, which assumes the danger is gone when the perpetrator 'calms down'. Control and manipulation are more sophisticated methods to employ, more sophisticated than merely hitting someone into submission, and so may present the perpetrator as more culpable and guilty. 'Losing control' is a behaviour many people can relate to and is easier to forgive. The perpetrator is manipulative and will use his manipulation on professionals and those close to the victim. This again is very different to the man who 'honestly' lost his temper in a very public display of what can be perceived as natural (though not acceptable) violence. Manipulation is hidden and dishonest. It does not sit comfortably with discourses of hetero/masculinity. In this respect resistance to the dominant discourse is significant indeed, and actually requires us to challenge deeply embedded beliefs about gender and hetero/sexuality. It is women who are discursively constructed as dishonest, not men. This turns some beliefs on their heads and often provokes a defence of masculinity. However, it is a relatively small percentage of men who display these characteristics in Western culture and this should be considered; not all men are abusers.

Victims of abuse are popularly perceived to be the barrier to implementing a robust criminal justice deterrent. They may be perceived as reckless for failing to leave the abuser, or they may be seen as weak and incapable of managing their situation. However, ending the relationship rarely ends the abuse, in fact research shows us that ending the relationship can increase the danger and the abuse exponentially (Websdale 2010, Richards 2010, Stark 2007). The biggest barrier, in reality, to the implementation of a robust criminal justice deterrent is not the victim, it is the *abuser*, and the people he can control; those people include professionals, not just frontline police, but also health practitioners, judges, magistrates, coroners, and council and government officials.

So if we are going to accept that coercion and control are the real dominant characteristics of abuse, and violence is just one method of control, we are constructing a counter discourse. This is no small exercise. For example, we will argue in this book that women who are the focus for abuse are very often skilled managers; the person in the victim's life who can offer the most safety is the abuser, not necessarily the police; the men who abuse are often dangerously dependent, obsessive and fearful; and the abuse is a pattern of pernicious and grievous control. Suggesting that abusers are dependent does not also suggest that they are benign or not dangerous. A need to control another out of fear because you are dependent on them can be manifested in violent or deeply abusive behaviours. Similarly, fear does not always inspire the victim to lose agency. Most people acting through fear will take the route they see as most likely to preserve their life. In domestic abuse this may be to do whatever the abuser wants or dictates, and that is still a strategy, it is still a resistance to power when it has a pragmatic function. If this was seen as the true picture for a typical domestic abuse situation of IPA, would we employ the same strategies to deal with it? Would we employ the strategies we have in the same way? Would we be better able to recognise abuser and abused? Would we be able to raise its status?

We will, in this chapter, begin to resist the dominant discourse and explore the new discursive truths of domestic abuse and IPA. We will begin with the abuse itself as this is the context in which the abuser and abused exist.

Domestic Abuse Case Study 3: Jenny

Jenny called the police one night because she was terrified her partner was going to kill her. He had put his hands around her throat and squeezed. There were no marks but the police arrested him for assault and he was taken to a police station.

Jenny gave the police a statement and disclosed a long history of assaults, including being beaten with a weapon, and other strangulation assaults, one of which caused her to pass out. As the assaults were historical there was no evidence with which to charge her partner.

Police conducted a risk assessment. They spoke with Jenny about the abuse she was experiencing. Only eight of the boxes were ticked.

What do you think should happen in this case?

What actually happened: Jenny was assessed as medium risk so did not get referred to the MARAC (MARAC is Multi Agency Risk Assessment Conference and is a panel to consider safety planning for high risk victims). Her partner was released with a caution, and no referral was made to a women's support service, despite Jenny giving her permission for a referral to be made. The CPS thought there was insufficient evidence to pursue a charge and, as this was his first offence, a caution was deemed the best outcome. The officer filling out the risk assessment did not have the skills to recognise that this was a high risk case, irrespective of the number of ticks achieved on the form. The process for referral by the police was inefficient and poorly resourced. This outcome could have increased the danger for Jenny, who says she will never ask for support again.

Re-writing the abuse

The definition

So, apart from refining what constitutes abuse, the new definition expands to include young people between the ages of 16 and 18 as victims. This group of women and girls are disproportionately affected by abuse and violence in their relationships. It is reported that there is a worrying trend of very young women reporting violence in their relationships, with a quarter reporting victimisation (Bradbury-Jones and Taylor 2013). The new definition states that domestic abuse is:

> Any incident or pattern of incidents of controlling, coercive or threatening behaviour, violence or abuse between those aged 16 or over who are or have been intimate partners or family members regardless of gender or sexuality. This can encompass but is not limited to the following types of abuse:
>
> - psychological
> - physical
> - sexual
> - financial
> - emotional
>
> Controlling behaviour is: a range of acts designed to make a person subordinate and/or dependent by isolating them from sources of support, exploiting their resources and capacities for personal gain, depriving them of the means needed for independence, resistance and escape and regulating their everyday behaviour.
>
> Coercive behaviour is: an act or a pattern of acts of assault, threats, humiliation and intimidation or other abuse that is used to harm, punish, or frighten their victim.
>
> This definition, which is not a legal definition, includes so-called'honour' based violence, female genital mutilation (FGM) and forced marriage, and is clear that victims are not confined to one gender or ethnic group. (Home Office 2012)

So, domestic abuse as defined is not at this time written into law as a specific criminal offence. The law responds to domestic abuse using existing crimes of assault and, more recently, harassment and so-called stalking. The behaviours which constitute *coercive control*, or even coercion and control, do not always, on their own or indeed together, infract the criminal law. So, a criminal justice response at this time, in the UK and many other places, is inhibited. This does not mean that those behaviours are not dangerous. Controlling men are identified as presenting the highest risk for killing their intimate partner or former intimate partner, irrespective of whether they are also habitually violent In fact, Stark (2013) reports that coercive control is a higher risk than violence alone by a factor of 9:1. So-called domestic homicide kills more women than any other form of homicide (this is discussed in Chapter 4). There has been much research which tells us what the typical IPF perpetrator is like, and risk assessment tools are in common use by police and other services in the UK, Canada, the USA, and many other places, to assess the danger of homicide in domestic abuse calls. Identifying risk should not be the biggest issue in terms of what we know, but that knowledge is not being absorbed adequately by professionals at every level of the justice system, so high risk victims are not always being identified or supported. The bigger problem is actually responding to risk effectively and providing ongoing safety planning, which covers all agencies, including police, magistrates and judges, coroners, lawyers, housing, financial and health practitioners.

There are many innovations and interventions in domestic abuse management but many are not adequately supported throughout the system. The police are an organisation which receives the bulk of criticism for not responding well to IPA. Many other organisations respond appallingly to victims of abuse but do not receive any public criticism. Some professionals, like prosecutors, coroners or judges, do not receive half the pressure they should do to acquire skills in recognising and responding to domestic abuse. The police and victims are let down at many stages in the system. A recent HMIC (2014) report into police responses to domestic abuse highlighted many areas where the police are failing. Whilst this report was necessary and timely, more scrutiny of the support from other areas is also necessary. Multi-agency domestic homicide reviews (DHRs) routinely highlight poor practice across the services, including housing and health.

The tertiary response, which is what happens after a homicide or arrest, needs far more attention and pressure to improve. For example, police may arrest a perpetrator and convince a victim to support a prosecution, then a judge or magistrate whose knowledge is from a position within a dominant discourse of abuse, may not support the position of the police or victim. This may leave the victim in more danger than she was in before she agreed to support a prosecution. Media also have a role to play, they have a specific agenda, which is not necessarily to make victims or communities safer. Media isolate stories of domestic homicide from each other and report cases drawing from knowledge produced in dominant discourses (Monckton Smith 2012), they routinely fail to link cases or to inform the public of specific risk factors.

Often, because domestic abuse is not a so-called black letter criminal offence, there may be no criminal justice intervention, and a woman may be referred to another agency for help after an emergency call, especially where no criminal offence can be identified, or police have failed to identify it. These are all difficult and dangerous actions for her, which do not always protect her from further harm, abuse or contact with the perpetrator; especially where she is forced to have some contact via child access for example. There are also those situations where the woman does not wish to leave the perpetrator at that time, for many reasons, and just wants him to stop the abuse. For many women the repercussions of taking any action which appears to indicate she may leave, or that she is receiving help or influence from others, may be devastating (discussed further in Chapter 6). In this respect she is playing her ace card and if she is let down at this point the repercussions may be fatal. However, women who will not support criminal or civil prosecution, are described as frustrating and reckless, and the abuser is no longer seen as the problem, she is. It would be more useful for police, judges, magistrates and other frontline services to work with the victim's strategy as part of her ongoing safety planning, and not focus on their own strategy, which is often not adequately resourced, structurally supported throughout the process, or historically successful. Stanko (cited in Hoyle and Palmer 2014:192) argues that services should respond with support for the needs and desires of the victim, irrespective of whether they fit with an organisational agenda. Walklate and Mythen (2011) similarly argue that a response that does not work with the woman's perception of the danger she is in and how to manage that danger, is dangerous for the victim. It is also the case that, apart from not working with the woman's strategy, criminal justice services are not even working to a shared agenda. The CPS have a separate agenda to the police, judges and magistrates have another position, coroners, the media and healthcare have differing agendas again. There is no multi-agency joined up response or clear care pathway that police or victims can rely on when they are making decisions about the woman's future at a point of first contact, or in an emergency situation. Multi-agency hubs are being used in many places now and creating a forum where different agencies can share information. But a stated shared agenda, and interagency training may help support the success of this kind of innovation (Szilassy et al. 2014).

Police complain that they can never predict what individual judges, magistrates or juries will do; consequently they can make no promises to the victim. Or worse, they do make promises which cannot be delivered. This suggests that the criminal justice response cannot be the main response, a clearer pathway for the victim, so that she can make informed decisions with some certainty of outcome, is necessary. It is the case, and we discuss this later in Chapter 9, that poor practice is causing the failure of some good policy. As noted, interagency training may be helpful in this regard to give frontline responders and others, a good knowledge of what resources there are, what they do and how they can support each other. Research has shown that professionals have more confidence to speak with victims and take action after interagency training (Szilassy et al. 2014).

We have focused on the perceptions of frontline police and paramedics in our interviews. Police and paramedics have a job to do, and that job is separate from the context of the incident they are attending. For example, paramedics are there to deal with medical issues and injury, police are there to identify if any offences have been committed and who the offenders are, they also have a duty to protect life and property. They are not equipped in their processes or remit, to provide ongoing support and the victim knows this; so does the abuser. Hester (2013a) suggests that victims are using the system to manage the immediate crisis, to stop immediate violence, and to manage an imminent threat. And this is actually what the frontline police can offer, the victim has made a sensible cost/benefit analysis and assessment of police intervention as it currently works. So when ongoing action is suggested, victims do not always feel ready, especially in a crisis situation, to decide to make the life altering, and life threatening, decision to leave and challenge the abuser. Kirby et al. (2014) suggests that victims are more pragmatic about when and how to leave, and often this will not be a knee-jerk reaction to violence. They need time and space and support to form a realistic safety plan. Pain reports that 'while people who are abused adopt skills of precaution and management to try and maintain security for themselves and their children, domestic abuse is not something that you "get used to". The fear and trauma that interviewees talk about continue, and often intensify, over months or years' (2013:10), Pain also states that the fear is rational and justified (2014), which suggests that the threats to the victim are real, not imagined. Professionals do not always seem to fully appreciate that both her fear and her response are rational.

There is, of course, another situation, one where the woman has sought no help, or cannot seek help, and is existing with the perpetrator in a toxic environment. Other family members may identify this, or friends or colleagues, but there is no possible intervention with the current model and current thinking. In these situations, especially where there is no violence reported or observed, the victim has few options for support. The abuse is a *course of conduct.* It often spans many years. The victim will be trained to be frightened. And she has good reason to be frightened as this is, statistically, the biggest and most viscerally real, violent threat to her life she will ever suffer. Frontline responders should recognise the extent to which her fear is genuine and supported by research evidence. Pain (2013) found that keeping someone in a state of chronic fear does not require the use of regular, or even any, violence and that, in line with what we have found, victims are not passive and are managing the abuse with considerable courage and strength.

What the abuse looks like in reality

We think that to properly appreciate what abuse looks like from the inside the language of everyday terrorism is compelling, it captures the way fear, rather than violence, dominates the lives of the victims of abuse. Chronic fear is not the same as immediate fear, and there are misunderstandings in this respect. Immediate fear may dissipate when the immediate threat is gone. Chronic fear persists and grows and is made worse with every new 'immediate threat' and the ongoing nature of the abuse. Pain states that Judith Herman's (1997) 'classic account of trauma links the experiences of survivors of violent atrocities including torture, concentration camps and family violence. She argues that complex trauma arises from a setting from which escape is difficult, and a perpetrator who may appear "normal"' (cited in Pain 2013:11). The discourse of everyday terrorism focuses on the role of fear (Pain 2014) and how it traps women, not only in the spatial confines of the home but also within the political confines of femininity. Pain (2014) notes that Foucault's ideas of panopticism, the idea of self-regulation because you don't know when you're being watched, is the perfect analogy for the outputs of chronic fear.Panopticism is useful in comprehending the abuser's total surveillance, so that everything the victim has or is, is vulnerable, and that she will police herself all the time, never knowing whether she is being watched or not. She cannot let her guard slip. Often, women who are victims will deny abuse and declare love for the abuser even when he is not there. Many professionals do not understand this. They are not differentiating between a standard fear of an immediate threat, and a chronic fear and dread, which never go away.

One of the most compelling visual illustrations developed to show the way domestic abuse works is the Duluth power and control wheel, which has been in use in victim and abuser/batterer programmes since the 1990s (Pence and Paymar 1993). It is used in 50 states in the USA and in 17 countries (Gondolf 2010). It shows how violence is only part of the story of abuse, and often not the biggest part, but that control is multi-faceted and touches every part of the victim's life. The wheel has its critics and anti-feminist rhetoric plays some part. However, there is little doubt that the wheel has had a significant effect, especially in educating women about abuse. It is the case that women do not always recognise they are abused. They will justify and excuse violence against them, and it has also been noted that direct questions about whether they are abused may be met with a negative. Sometimes they don't feel worthy of the label of domestic abuse victim, sometimes they feel it is disempowering or shameful. But women will often recognise different kinds of abuse as happening to them when specific examples are given (Thurston et al. 2009). Some women describe their first contact with the Duluth wheel as the most empowering thing that has ever happened to them (Monckton Smith 2010).

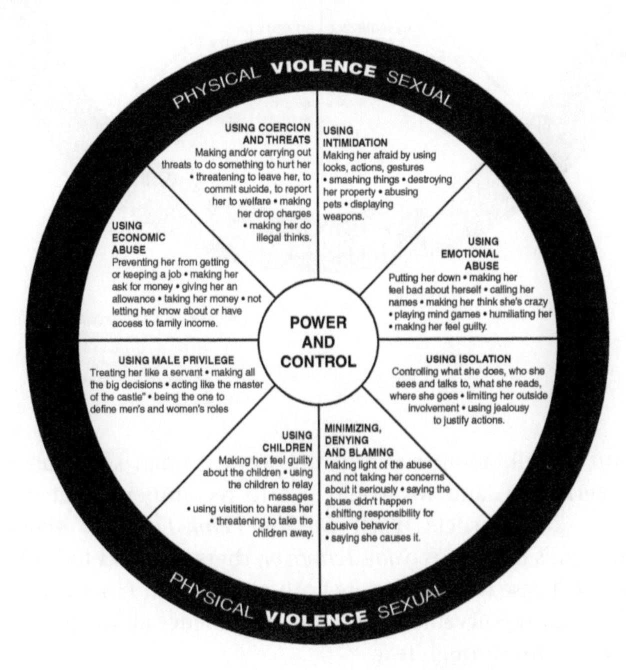

DOMESTIC ABUSE INTERVENTION PROJECT
202 East Superior Street
Duluth, Minnesota 55802
218-722-2781

Whereas the equality wheel depicts the characteristics of a healthy relationship:

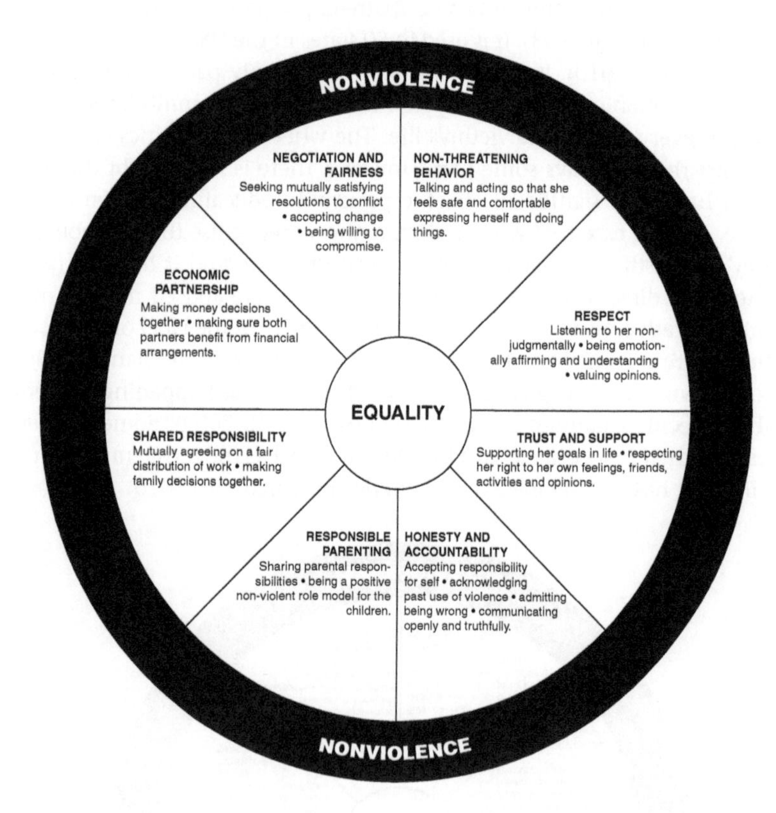

We want to talk about some of the ways women suffer abuse and everyday terrorism, and we would like to recommend that you read Sweetnam's (2013) article *Where Do You Think Domestic Abuse Hurts Most*? and Pain's (2013) *Everyday Terrorism*, there are links to both in the reference list. These two articles are both powerful and instructive. They capture how abuse, surveillance, threat and violence all work together to control the victim through fear.

We should take some time to look at some of the behaviours recorded from our experience and research as used often by abusive men. There will be multiple behaviours, and they will be in play most of the time. Many of these behaviours will not be recognised by outsiders, or not witnessed by them, or may be misinterpreted by them; so we will look at these three types of situational examples of what the victim may be experiencing. Each victim's experience will be somewhat different. It should also be remembered that abuse is a *course of conduct* and it would be easy to dismiss some of these behaviours as trivial when viewed in isolation. Abuse is ongoing, it is cumulative in terms of the fear produced and will include multiple methods of control and humiliation. The victim is trained to be afraid and in a constant state of dread. The idea of everyday terrorism is brought into sharp relief when the following list is considered in that context:

Not witnessed by outsiders – but commonly used:

Threats to children of the victim
Forced intimate examination to check for alleged sexual activity
Checking the house for dust or cleanliness
Leading around the house by her hair
Insisting on a certain order for placing items on shelves or in a cupboard
Surveillance of electronic equipment like phone or computer
Physical surveillance, like keeping the toilet door open, with little opportunity for privacy
Following from room to room
Punishments for breaking the rules set by the abuser
Silence and staring
Food or drink being taken away or restricted
Complaints about food and cooking
Standing closely over her whilst she completes a task
Sitting on top of her so she can't move
Restricting the amount of toilet paper which can be used
Money being restricted and monitored
Mileage being checked on the car
Petrol levels checked against mileage
Markers put on the tyres for signs of movement
Restricted use of the phone
Cameras in the home
Bugging equipment in the home
No go areas in the home
Denigrating her monthly cycle
Threats to her children, friends or family
Denigrating her family and friends

Timing her in tasks or outside activities
Threats to pets
Holding her by the throat and smiling

Stalking is often used both in relationships which have ended and in relationships which are current. Stalking from a distance can be very menacing and behaviours include:

Following from a distance and randomly
Standing outside the house staring
Breaking into the house and moving things or leaving things behind
Damage to property which seems small and trivial
Breaking in and pouring water onto the bed
Constant phoning or texting
Standing outside her children's school
Suddenly and unexpectedly being in a place
Leaving messages which can be overtly threatening, or may be sinister in a way only recognised by the victim

Behaviours not recognised:

> These are behaviours which hold special meaning for the victim and are a sign that her behaviour is unacceptable and things are beginning to escalate, or will escalate later in private. These signs work because they are related to chronic fear. Specific examples from our interviews with victims are given in Chapter 6. When the victim sees this sign she will often change her behaviour and rely on her safety strategy. For example, a trigger for escalated fear or dread can come from a key phrase or word unknown to others, a specific facial expression like raising an eyebrow to give warning, starting to laugh at her, frowning; it will be personal to that woman and the result of history. Outsiders will not recognise these signs, but they will have a relationship to deeply abusive or violent actions for the victim. She may find it impossible to function confidently after such a sign, or may start to deny things she has said or done. She may demonstrate loyalty to the abuser and appear to turn against those trying to help her. She thinks that no one else will be able to keep her safe. One woman reported to us that one night at a party she wet herself with fear after her boyfriend saw her talking to another man and started grinding his teeth. No one else noticed.

Behaviours which can be misinterpreted as loving or normal:

Constant hand holding; can be controlling and a sign to others to stay away (some more violent men may squeeze her hand to control her, causing varying amounts of pain, or just pressure to make sure she behaves)
Never arguing (there may be no allowance for disagreement)
Always together (never allowed to be on her own)
Constant texting or calling, not necessarily loving; can be surveillance
Restricting the type of clothes she can wear (you look like a tart in that or it makes me jealous)
Complaining about, or banning the use of make-up (you look much better without make-up, you don't need that muck on your face, women who wear make-up are sluts)
Encouraged to wear provocative clothing, then criticism of the clothes
Excessive jealousy (he loves her so much he can't stand other men to look at her)
Violence (he loves her so much she has this strong effect on him)
Threatening others who talk to her (he's so protective)
I want my chips done this way (is not about preference, it is control and threat)

These are just examples, and different types of control, strategy and abuse will involve different types of behaviours. It is, however, often the case that particularly female roles, behaviours and expectations will be targeted for abuse. Like, for example, cooking, housekeeping, childcare, monthly cycle, make-up, clothing, obedience, sexual behaviour, pregnancy and weight. This is integral to dominant discourses of hetero/sexuality. An abuser will attack anything traditionally or stereotypically 'feminine' to control the victim, or crush her self-esteem and room for action (Stark 2013). As a result of cultural, social and religious codes of practice and tradition, it is particularly 'feminine' behaviours which are the most easily controlled. This is for many reasons, but one of the most important is the structural supports in place that facilitate and excuse abusive behaviours with this focus, and the politics of femininity. Stark states that:

> coercive control takes the enforcement of gender stereotypes as its specific aim, the degradation of femininity as a major means, and reinforces sexual inequality in society as a whole in ways that constrain women's opportunities to 'do' femininity, it is about the construction and deconstruction of gender identity in ways that other forms of violence against women are not. (2009:1512)

For example, controlling the use of make-up can appear reasonable since make-up wearing is often denigrated, so there is some solidarity with the abuser. Also, make-up is closely related to sexual behaviour and is a cultural and religious norm to place controls on female sexuality (Benson and Stangroom 2009, Tanenbaum 2007, Kelly et al. 2005, Lees 1997). An example of a support which exists for this is the existence of words which are specifically used to denigrate women who are seen as promiscuous, like, for example, *slut, whore* or *slag*. Sue Lees' (1997) research into the use of the word 'slag', and discourses of heterosexuality, to control the behaviour of young women and girls in schools, shows how being labelled as a slag has repercussions, and is serious enough for girls to want to avoid the label. Tanenbaum found that nothing had changed in 2007 when she researched reputation. A 'slag' is a discursive subject, which could not exist as a wholly negative 'type' without some constructed belief that the behaviours which constitute being a slag are wrong, bad or even evil. The discursive subject which is the slag, exists in dominant discourses of gender, femininity and hetero/sexuality, and even where these truths are resisted they still have repercussions and effect (Tanenbaum 2007, Allen 2003, Lees 1997). So, using the word slag for a woman for wearing 'too much' make-up can invoke significant cultural and historical baggage, where the person so labelled is breaking the rules of culture as well as the rules of the abuser. This then is giving a nasty insult to exert control, the weight and gravitas of cultural, societal and religious solidarity with his position (Stark 2009, Tanenbaum 2007, Lees 1997). This is the position with many female roles and behaviours, if she is breaking the 'feminine code', then he, as a man, has support for his desire to bring her back in line (Monckton Smith 2012, Stark 2009). Much of the time these dominant discourses are part of a discursive formation, where these truths are shared across powerful institutions. This is institutional sexism where some people will inadvertently facilitate abuse by supporting that sexism. There is also much support for traditional masculinity within these dominant discourses, and men are excused routinely for using violence and expressing extreme jealousy as a normal output of hetero/masculinity (Monckton Smith 2012). It should also be remembered that this is also an effective method of controlling men, and the cause of distress for them which could produce abusive behaviour, or be used to abuse them. Denigrating a man because he is not 'masculine' enough is a powerful stressor.

There is a message that any man could be an abuser; this may be true, any man *could* be an abuser because the structural supports, and victim vulnerability, are already there to help him (Stark 2009). But the truth is that *not all men are abusers*. Abusers are a sub group of men who are unable to deal with rejection, or feel powerless without total control, or have sociopathic or psychopathic traits, or have status issues. These men are far more likely to be the most dangerous kind of abuser (Websdale 2010, Brown et al. 2010). He is not everyman. So we must stop giving him excuses based on the idea that his abuse is linked to being a 'normal enough bloke'. We accept that his behaviour may be linked to political masculinity and the pressures of gender expectations, but it should not to be considered normal masculine behaviour. It's not. Gadd (2012) discusses domestic abuse prevention after the high profile case of serial abuser Raoul Moat who shot his former partner and killed her new partner. He also shot and blinded a police officer who later committed suicide (BBC 2012). Moat's violent control and dysfunction was almost invisible in the face of the accusations that his former partner had created his distress. Gadd (2012) suggests that most men do not abuse their partners, but those who do form a sizeable minority. It has been suggested in some research that abusers could form about ten per cent of the male population (Lonsway 2006).

The perfect victim

We want to now consider the discursive subject that is the victim of abuse. Dominant discourses of domestic abuse, hetero/sexuality, gender and romantic love all intersect to construct a version of reality which tells us who the victim of abuse is; what she looks like, her history, how she behaves and how she responds to abuse. So we already have some knowledge of a 'real' abuse victim. But we draw first from Nils Christie's (1986) idea of the perfect *crime* victim and then consider how a coercively controlled victim of everyday terrorism may differ. An ideal or perfect victim is said to have six key attributes:

1. She is weak
2. She is carrying out a respectable project at the time of victimisation
3. She is not to be blamed
4. There is a big bad offender
5. The offender is unknown to victim
6. She is powerful enough to make the offending known to others and claim herself to be a victim without threatening strong countervailing interests. (Van Wijk2013)

This is not merely a theoretical academic exercise, it has a very real practical application and policy implication. So we address the picture of the perfect violence victim and how she may differ from the coercively controlled victim. The coercively controlled victim challenges some of these victim attributes. She may use violence herself, she may abuse alcohol or drugs, she may be antagonistic to police, she may withdraw her complaints of assault, she may refuse to leave the abuser, she may shout and scream, she may just declare love for the abuser. All of these things do not inspire sympathy. But just because we don't sympathise with her, does not mean she is not a victim, and in a dangerous or potentially life threatening situation. A focus on whether she is worthy enough, is not addressing the real problem, which is him, and will reduce her status. So we will take each of the six attributes which we discursively link with being a *real* victim and show how they undermine the coercively controlled victim. We will talk about each attribute in the context of a police call for support after violence, which is when it is easiest to compare the abuse victim with other types of victim:

1. *She is weak*: weakness is allowed in respect of an assault. By this we mean the victim is physically weaker than the abuser. But weak also implies that she cannot, and indeed should not, use violence herself, and should be traumatised in a way that means she is crying and non-threatening. Where an abuser claims that a victim has used violence herself the anti-feminist argument of bilateral violence is often invoked (Flood 2009, Kimmel 2008). For example 'they're as bad as each other', and this makes her culpable. Weakness also implies that the victim will be crying and meek, and will also be grateful for the attendance of the police. A controlled victim may be intoxicated or difficult; many abuse victims self-medicate with alcohol, and have mental health distress. She may have been manipulated into intoxication, distress or anger by the abuser so that she appears to be the problem on the arrival of the police. She may also refuse the help offered, but this is often strategy not recklessness. Weakness must be feminine weakness: physically weaker, non-violent, submissive and compliant.
2. *Respectable project*: for women this will mean she is doing something that is acceptable to her gender when she is victimised. So if an assault happens whilst she is at home looking after the children, or visiting her family, or shopping, she will have more victim status than if she was out drinking with her friends or in the company of another man. Not being respectable has been used as an excuse over and again to justify male violence and homicide. This is starkly illustrated with,so-called, honour violence. If a man claims he was pushed to attack her by her flirting, or infidelity, she will not be a proper victim and he will be excused. Often, men who kill their partners will claim a

'crime of passion' and the suspicion that she was having an affair. This has caused great problems in criminal justice terms where the excuse has been over-used and over-successful. It is (allegedly) more difficult now to make this claim. Even where there is a clear history of control and abuse the 'crime of passion' claim still works (Monckton Smith 2012).

3. *She is not to be blamed*: she must not have provoked the response of violence or harassment, for example, and this will often be related to feminine codes of behaviour. When others assess her victim status, all too often unconscious or institutional sexism routinely influences the assessment. For example, she should not argue with him or shout (she knows what he's like), she must not hit out at him, she must not make him jealous, she must keep the home tidy, she must keep the children under control, there are many behaviours scrutinised in her, rather than in him, to rationalise the abuse or violence. Lees (1997) characterises these blameworthy behaviours in women as being 'naggers, whores or libbers'.
4. *There is a big bad offender*: he is one dimensionally bad and has used the type of violence on her which is unacceptable to other men. For example, he has used a fist rather than an open handed slap. He is a bully and unreasonable. If he is seen to be reasonable or plausible or, most importantly, loving, her victim status is reduced. Abusers are rarely this one dimensional, and controlling abusers are manipulators who can use the victim against herself, and appeal to dominant beliefs about the problems men have with 'difficult' women.
5. *The offender is unknown to the victim*: this is difficult, for in domestic abuse the offender is always known to the victim, so she can never achieve ideal victim status in this respect
6. *She is powerful enough to make the offending known to others and claim herself to be a victim without threatening strong countervailing interests:* she needs to be able to stand up and identify herself as a victim to others, especially the police, and allow them to use the criminal justice system to punish the offender for her. But she should not be angry, vengeful or vindictive. She must not overplay her hand, but be a compliant tool for prosecution by others in her interests. The victim status must not be a threat to the norms of society, and this is particularly difficult in domestic abuse. The criminal justice system is extraordinarily reluctant to criminalise men who appear to be acting within certain (quite far reaching) boundaries of 'normal' masculine behaviour or heteronormativity, and the privacy of domestic abuse is still jealously guarded in many spheres.

We have discussed her in relation to a violent incident, which is the type of incident most easily responded to by police. If we tried to discuss her in the context of control with no violence, it would be almost impossible to raise her to the status of victim at all, let alone perfect victim within this dominant discourse. The victim of domestic abuse challenges all of these traditional requirements, professionals do seem to adhere to this model when assessing how much sympathy they have for the victim, and how much they believe she is actually a victim and not just a trouble causer. It is also often the case that sympathy is expressed for the abuser where she does not conform to this model for victimhood.

Re-writing the victim of domestic abuse

As a cultural norm across the world we don't really like to give women too much freedom and choice. It is not just men who impose that belief, women do too. Mothers and female friends, female onlookers and commentators, will impose strict behavioural codes for other women. Foucault argues that power is not top down, it circulates, and is exercised and resisted at every level. Men *and* women impose restrictions on women. It is normal to place controls, especially romantic, domestic or sexual controls, on women. This makes it very difficult to rewrite the domestic abuse victim in a way which makes her wholly acceptable. This is because the abuse imposed on her is *control* and, discursively, it is actually the *degree of control* rather than control itself that is more or less acceptable. If we were to talk about the controlled victim as a human subject, rather than a female subject, it would be so much easier. There are many forms of control that will be used in domestic abuse. For example, violence is used as a form of control. This is more or less acceptable depending on the degree of violence used, what it was in response to, and which gender was using the violence. Getting the woman to use violence in front of others, or to leave a mark on the abuser, or to make it appear that she used violence, is a method of control just as surely as using violence on her is. This tactic is routinely used to undermine the victim's status as a victim. The abuse has to be assessed using a history, not a single incident. Female abuse victims are being criminalised and re-abused by the system. One of our interviewees told us that she was being hit by her husband one night and managed to call the police. He continued to beat her, but it was she who was witnessed hitting him when she finally managed to give him a slap in self-defence. She was scared and stressed, he was calm and plausible. She was arrested, criminalised, and lost custody of the children when they split. He did not have a record for violence. He laughs at her about this incident. The police did not have the training or knowledge of domestic abuse to assess the situation properly. Just one repercussion of this is that the children now live with a violent abuser (see Chapter 7).

So the victim is being routinely controlled. She has been trained to be frightened, she has been trained to behave in a certain way. If she was not frightened there would be no control. She is controlled and she is frightened and this fear is argued, in research, to be both rational and justified (Pain 2013:6), so it would be short-sighted to think of her as weak or reckless. She is managing a very dangerous man on a day to day basis, she is keeping herself safe, and in many cases alive, by her actions. For this chapter our purpose is to present the idea that the victim of abuse does not lose her ability to assess risk, or to protect herself. She is not always hysterical or reckless in choosing the path she does. The victim of abuse is often choosing a path, or strategy, which will keep her safe. Her fear of the abuser does not always match her faith in the police or the system to protect her.

So this victim is not ideal. She may self-medicate, she may have alcohol or substance abuse problems. In any other situation where such abuse and trauma are present we would expect to see these issues. She is likely to have mental health problems, she will probably present as far more problematic than him in an emergency call. The call hasn't been made because he is frightened or confused; she is frightened and confused. It is unreasonable, if not ridiculous, to expect that anyone in fear would be able to be plausible and helpful when the cause of that fear is still present and still threatening.

Re-writing the abuser

The discursively constructed abuser is just as difficult to resist. They may never have used violence, and this makes it very difficult to be perceived as dangerous within current beliefs. We can understand a woman cowering from a fist or a knife. When we can't see or hear stereotypical threats we assume there is no threat and that the victim is either dishonest or hysterical. Coercive control is used to maintain control over the woman, and we must cultivate a better understanding of why some men *need* such control. It is not that all these men are evil, most present as perfectly ordinary individuals, but a better understanding of *his* dependence on her, rather than seeing her as dependent on him, could create more imaginative strategies for intervention. Research, such as that from Neil Websdale (2010) and Evan Stark (2007), has suggested that perpetrators are often dependent on the woman, and the conjugal family unit, for their own sense of identity or worth. This dependence has been cited as present in cases of familicide, domestic abuse and domestic homicide. Societal norms, which pressure men to be a certain way and create unrealistic expectations about their own status, cannot be isolated from domestic abuse and homicide.

Brown et al. (2010) talk about the 'rejection model' for understanding why some perpetrators abuse their partners. This model certainly fits well with the stories told by some of the victims in our research. Brown et al. found that the more controlling men were, the less they were able to deal with their partner's autonomy or difference. A cycle of rejection and abuse, they say, could account for some men's intractability when it comes to domestic abuse.

They describe the cycle in the following terms:

1. The man experiences rejection
2. Man perceives it as shaming or a threat to his ego
3. Man defends himself from the threat
4. Physical or psychological abuse follows

The abuser needs emotional closeness or alleviation of distress to defend himself from the threat, but often the opposite results as he tries to punish the victim for creating the threat, or force her into declaring her devotion to him. The abuse is an attack on the person from whom he wants affirmation. Abusers have emotional and psychological problems, and perpetrator programmes that focus only on showing how abuse is wrong and do not address the psychological disturbance and dysfunction, may not be as successful as those that do. Often the female victim recognises this cycle and knows how to respond to it; she must declare love and devotion, even if being beaten, and especially in the presence of others, like the police (see Chapter 7).

A man who is managing distress because he feels he is losing control of a woman he is dependent on, is not going to respond well to an intervention which appears to pull her further from him. He will use many methods to maintain or exert control, which may include: violence, including homicide; begging and pleading; punishment of the victim in a number of ways, convincing the victim she is in the wrong; removing anyone who could influence her to leave; threatening those she loves so she feels she needs to protect them by staying away from them; and so on. Every crisis, if not handled with care, can make the situation worse. There is a need for perpetrator programmes which intervene and address the psychological problems of the abuser. In the long run it will be cheaper and more effective to focus some attention on him. He will be a serial abuser, even if the current victim is made safe, he will move on to another who will need help. The problem is not her, it is him.

Brown et al. (2010) suggest that his need for control is more than a masculine enactment of patriarchal power. The sense of entitlement which is said to be an output of patriarchy might be better understood as justifying and excusing the control, and not necessarily the reason for it.

Brown et al. suggest that programmes or interventions address: loss of power, internal arousal to violence, and strategies to handle conflict. Other problems which may also be addressed include: self-awareness, personal responsibility, problem solving, rights of others and anger management. Brown et al. argue that abuse is about attachment anxiety, and links between shame and violence. They say that men need to become more resistant to rejection to avoid feeling overwhelmed, and they need to confront issues of shame. Perpetrator or batterer programmes have been in use for some time, however, they are not as universal as programmes for victims. Most perpetrator programmes are court mandated, with fewer places for men who might self-refer. There is not a clear sense of responsibility placed on abusers to address their behaviour, the discourse presents the woman as holding the responsibility to stop the abuse, or remove herself from its environs, rather than the man to stop abusing.

Perpetrator programmes have a high level of attrition, between 15 per cent and 58 per cent (Jewell and Wormith 2010). It is also the case that studies have shown that there is only a small reduction in violence afterwards. This could be associated with the suggestion that the characteristics which predict serial abuse in men, are the same characteristics which predict failure to complete a programme (Jewell 2010). So those characteristics need to be examined, and perhaps more flexibility given in programme delivery. Jewell (2010) reports that the predictors for not completing a programme are:

1. Lower age
2. Lower SE status
3. Unemployment
4. Lower education
5. Unmarried

6. Substance abuse
7. Anti-social personality
8. Violence in history
9. History of abuse
10. Severity of assaults
11. Previous arrests

In conclusion, Jewell (2010) found that court mandated programmes are more likely to be completed, and that those with the most to lose are the most likely to complete. However, the characteristics which predict recidivism and failure to complete also predict higher risk for homicide. These groups should be targeted for programmes which address their dysfunction. It is beginning to be more widely accepted that anti-social personality disorders, depressive illness, psychopathy and psychosis are all associated with homicide. Echeburua and Fernandez-Montalvo (2007:254) categorise abusers into three groups: family only, dysphoric/borderline, and generally violent/anti-social. It is suggested that the anti-social group constitute 25 per cent of abusers, and these men will indulge in violence in and out of the domestic relationship, will have criminal records and mental health disorders like psychopathy. They often have hostile attitudes to women, and the highest rate of alcohol dependence. Personality disorders are often seen among perpetrators of domestic violence, the most commonly diagnosed being anti-social, borderline, and narcissistic (Hamberger& Hastings, 1988, 1991; Huss &Langhinrichsen-Rohling, 2000 cited in Echeburua and Fernandez-Montalvo 2007:254).

The new stalking law takes into consideration obsessive behaviours of perpetrators and this strategy could be usefully applied to domestic abusers, who are more often than not one and the same. It may be time to consider that the domestic abuser is not just any man. He is a man with a certain amount of dysfunction and an inability to cope with a range of life's challenges. His dysfunction is not labelled as such, but is discursively constructed as masculine, normal 'for a man' and understandable. His dysfunction is hidden behind societal acceptance that men may be violent, or excessively jealous as a normal output of masculine hetero/sexuality. It is time to rewrite the domestic abuser, not as an extreme version of the standard man, but as a man with serious and potentially dangerous dysfunction; dysfunction which can be hidden behind a plausible countenance. They need help, rather than punishment in isolation.

Domestic Abuse Case Study 4: Raoul Moat

Raoul Moat was a serial abuser who was imprisoned after violently abusing his child. Whilst in prison it was noted that Moat sent messages stating he was going to kill his former partner Samantha Stobbart. He was released from prison on 1 July 2010. On 3rd July he shot and killed Samantha's new partner Chris Brown, he then repeatedly shot Samantha Stobbart through a window, injuring, but not killing her. Moat then ran and managed to evade capture. On 4 July he shot a uniformed patrol officer, PC David Rathband, in the face, blinding him. This officer later killed himself. The police confirm on 5 July that Durham prison had informed them that Moat intended serious harm to his former partner. Moat was finally found on 10 July hiding out in the village of Rothbury. Moat apparently killed himself after a siege.

Moat's suffering was a key point for discussion, and when fellow abuser, former footballer Paul Gascoigne, turned up at the siege to talk to 'Moaty' and persuade him to give himself up (Gadd 2012) the whole story became trivialised and a serious discussion of Moat's similarity to many domestic abusers was lost. There remains a question over the release of a man from prison, whilst he is committing a serious offence (threats to kill), and why the police did not immediately take this seriously and help Samantha Stobbart to a position of safety. Three other men were arrested and convicted of assisting Moat in his mission to kill his former partner, her partner and the police officer. This kind of masculine solidarity structurally supports domestic abuse. This kind of solidarity was seen also in Case Study 1, the murder of Emily Longley by Elliott Turner. In a lot of media reporting domestic abuse was not mentioned, and Moat was represented as a violent atypical man. He was also hailed as a hero and a legend on many internet sites set up to venerate him.

4
The Problem of Domestic Abuse and Homicide

What do we know about domestic homicide?

The human cost

Domestic abuse and domestic homicide are closely related. Most domestic homicides are preceded by domestic abuse, and experts argue that they are predictable (Adams 2007). The worldwide scale of domestic abuse against women is staggering and in some countries up to 71 per cent of women will experience domestic abuse in their lifetime (Bradbury-Jones and Taylor 2013). In the UK the figure is believed to be 1 in 4, and 1 in 3 in Scotland, though Bradbury-Jones and Taylor urge caution when looking at these figures because domestic abuse is widely under-reported. The NSPCC (2014) report over 3,000 calls a year from adolescents experiencing violence in a relationship, and one in ten calls are from boys.

Domestic homicide, or more specifically for our purposes, intimate partner femicide (IPF), is a problem of substantial proportions on a global scale. Women across the world are being killed by their intimate partners, or former intimate partners, at significant rates. Women are at much greater risk than men of being murdered by an intimate partner, for example, statistics from the USA in 2002 show that of all the domestic homicides committed by a spouse, 81 per cent of the victims were wives; and of all those committed by a non-married intimate partner, 71 per cent of the victims were women (Chanmugam 2014). Women are nine times more likely to be killed by their intimate partner than by a stranger (Campbell et al. 2007) even though nearly all safety advice to women and girls focuses on stranger danger. IPV is also the most common cause of non-fatal injuries in women, and the biggest cause of traumatic death and injury in pregnant and post-partum women in the USA (Van Wormer and Roberts 2009). Research has shown that women are reluctant for many reasons to seek help from criminal justice agencies, but when they do they are not always seeking prosecution, they just want the abuse to stop (Hester 2013a). Many victims will have a history of accessing healthcare as a result of abuse. An American study found that 74 per cent of murdered women and 88 per cent of survivors had sought treatment for an IPV injury from emergency services in the previous year (Roehl et al. 2005). There are cases where the woman never discloses the abuse she is suffering, but it should be noted that domestic homicide almost never occurs out of the blue. A common misunderstanding is that a domestic homicide occurs as a result of a particularly heated argument where the man has accidentally 'lost it' and killed the woman in an incident that could not have been predicted. Many domestic homicides are represented this way in media reporting, and even in official forensic narratives (Monckton Smith 2012). This is a problem in itself as the risk to women of homicide from abuse are not fully understood, and therefore not responded to. When police, magistrates, judges, coroners, doctors, healthcare providers, social services, housing agencies and others all share the same dominant discursive construction of domestic abuse and homicide, it becomes the 'truth' of the problem. Juodis et al. (2014) and Adams (2007) argue that most domestic homicide involves planning and can be predicted. It is also inaccurate to assume that it is violence which best predicts domestic homicide, Stark (2013) reports that coercive control is a better predictor of domestic homicide by a ratio of 9:1. Domestic *abuse* is a term which better captures the risk and dangerous behaviours than the term domestic *violence*. Some use the term *everyday terrorism* to illustrate the fear and control involved in high risk abuse.

A history of domestic abuse is the biggest predictor for future abuse (Stark 2007), and men who abuse their partners are usually serial abusers. Two women a week are killed by current or former intimate partners in the UK (Hester 2009), three a day in the USA (VPC 2005), one every six hours in South Africa (Matthews et al. 2004), 5,000 a year in Pakistan (Chang 2010), and three a week in Spain (ABC 2010); it is the only category for homicide in which women predominate as victims. But these numbers do not capture the full extent of the problem, many domestic homicides are not classified as such, but are misinterpreted as, for example, car accidents, suicides, suicide pacts, accidents, sex games, and drug abuse. Wherever there has been a history of abuse and a sudden death occurs, homicide should always be considered. An Australian coroner even re-opened hundreds of cases after realising that many may have been given the wrong verdict (Passmore and Weston 2011). But apart from homicide deaths, the number of suicides by women who are known to suffer domestic abuse is even more alarming. Walby (2004) suggests that between four and ten women a week are committing suicide as a result of domestic abuse, these victims had all presented to an emergency department for IPV injury in the year prior to their death. These numbers do not count the large number of near misses routinely witnessed in emergency departments, nor the near fatal strangulation assaults which are often left untreated to protect the abuser. IPA is also the biggest cause of homelessness, mental health problems, and substance and alcohol abuse amongst women (Women's Aid 2014), and Stark (2013) states that abused women are 15 times more likely to abuse alcohol and nine times more likely to abuse drugs, they are also far more likely to commit suicide. Intimate partner abuse (IPA) is not a small problem. It is catastrophic for the abused women, expensive in both financial and human terms for our societies and communities, and creates a toxic and miserable existence for many children. In fact, Steeves and Parker (2007) report that in the USA between 3,000 and 4,000 children every year are affected by domestic homicide and many witness the murder, in fact it is suggested that children are more likely to witness the murder of their mother than be absent, or be killed themselves (cited in Chanmugam 2014: 74). Most domestic abuse occurs in front of children (Hester 2009).

The financial cost

It is estimated that each domestic homicide costs the criminal justice system over a million pounds (Richards 2006), Women's Aid (2014) report that domestic abuse costs the criminal justice system over three billion a year, and it represents three per cent of the National Health's budget, the cost to social services, housing authorities, mental health services and legal services is another billion pounds and it is the cause of much child abuse, neglect and death. In fact, Harne and Radford (2008) estimate the general costs to be around 23 billion pounds per annum. As discussed in Chapter 1, even though domestic abuse is often stated as a political priority by government, for all the reasons we have just given it still doesn't have the kind of status that attracts co-ordinated media, societal and cultural condemnation. The resistance to the dominant discourse is not universal, and counter discourses have been more thoroughly resisted in some contexts. It is not even a stated priority for all Police and Crime Commissioners. There are sometimes campaigns to raise awareness in the media, and these generate news articles and items that remind us of its prevalence. But what would be more effective is media support in the day to day reporting of homicide and abuse, where they don't rely on discourses of accident, or of a man being pushed too far by his wife's infidelity, or the tragedy of a couple killed in circumstances that leave everyone baffled. Adams (2007) argues that domestic homicides are predictable and that there is nearly always a history of control and abuse. This is rarely revealed by media reports that do not link domestic homicides, as they do with other crimes, to show patterns of behaviour (Monckton Smith 2012). Also, official forensic narratives often downplay or ignore the role of domestic abuse, which is actually central. The number one risk factor for domestic homicide is prior domestic abuse; it is male perpetrated domestic abuse that precipitates 65–70 per cent of cases where there is a female victim, and 75 per cent of cases where there is a male victim (Campbell et al. 2007).

So, we have to ask why we aren't managing to reduce the number of deaths of women. The number of men killed by their intimate partners has fallen dramatically in those places where interventions for domestic abuse have been put in place. The interventions currently employed seek to balance a criminal justice agenda of prosecution, and a societal agenda for the woman to leave the relationship with the use of refuges, mandatory arrest policies and so on. These interventions have reduced the number of deaths of men significantly as women see more choice and avoid violence as a last resort (Campbell et al. 2007). Reckdenwald and Palmer (2000) suggest that women's increased economic independence correlates with a decrease in male victim homicides as women have escape routes and financial independence and will generally choose a non-violent option to escape the abuser.

Prosecutions for domestic abuse and homicide related offending

Domestic violence conviction rates are at an all-time high with many more men pleading guilty (Hoyle and Palmer 2014). However, this does not mean that prosecutions are at an all-time high. It is still the case that most domestic abuse complaints do not result in CPS action and less than half of domestic abuse complaints achieve a conviction. Hester and Westmarland 2006 (cited in Gadd 2012: 504) found that in Northumbria only five per cent of reported incidents achieved an arrest, prosecution and conviction. Nelson (2014) reports from an American study that the best way to achieve a conviction for a domestic abuse crime is to make multiple charges. Nelson states that those charge sheets that had four offences had a 100 per cent conviction rate, whereas those with only one charge had a 29 per cent success rate. Nelson also reports that some 97 per cent of charges were resolved through plea bargaining. He holds that despite this apparent success domestic abuse arrests and prosecutions are still very low.

So there have been definite changes, but the prevalence of abuse of women is not decreasing, and the number of homicides of women has been fairly static for some time. In fact there is predicted to be a spike in domestic abuse and violence during the World Cup 2014, which is increasing for every tournament. Kirby et al. (2014) found that televised World Cup football increased the incidence of domestic violence by 26 per cent when England won, and 38 per cent when they lost. There was also an increase in recorded domestic abuse on the days following matches. The same patterns are noted following American soccer games. Bernhardt et al. argue (1998: 59, cited in Kirby et al. 2014: 262) that football fans identify with the teams and see their failures and successes as their own. Kirby et al. suggest this is encouraged when men gather together in pubs to watch matches on large screens and to drink alcohol at the same time. It is not only football tournaments that cause a rise in violence against women, but also other environmental and social factors, like times of high unemployment (Kirby et al. 2014).

So it seems that men are more willing to plead guilty (or are being forced to with the improvement in some frontline evidence gathering) but are still just as willing to indulge in domestic abuse. These two things together suggest a lack of shame in being labelled as an abuser. Research by Gadd et al. (2012) examined perpetrator responses to media which seeks to make us aware of what abuse is and what it looks like. They suggest that some perpetrators can identify quite strongly with discourses of the 'incorrigible perpetrator' and 'culpable victim'. Incorrigible suggests a rogue rather than a thug, for example, and there is societal understanding and even affection for masculine rogues. Domestic abuse may be frowned upon but there is still a long way to go before it is always seen as shameful for men. It is still associated with discourses of heteronormativity and standard masculinity, which justifies and excuses, even fatal, violence (Monckton Smith 2012).

However, it is important to remember that whilst any man could potentially indulge in abuse, given the structural supports which exist to facilitate it and the victim vulnerability to make it possible (Stark 2009), not all men do. Men who exert coercion and control, and those who go on to commit domestic homicide, are not just 'any man', they fall into broad categories and those who pose a high risk for homicide can often be identified (Adams 2007, Stark 2007). If we acknowledged more openly in forensic narratives and media reports the specificity of the domestic killer he may not receive such tacitly solid support from society and the criminal justice system.

Domestic Abuse Case Study 5: Mick Philpott

Philpott was found guilty of the manslaughter of six children in Derby in 2012. The six children were killed in a house fire Philpott, his wife Mairead and a friend of his, Paul Mosely, had deliberately set. The fire was an attempt to frame his former live-in girlfriend, Lisa Willis, for arson because she had 'dared to leave him' as the judge put it, and was on the eve of a custody hearing. He had lived in a polyamorous relationship with both Mairead and Lisa.

Philpott had a history of domestic abuse and had served three years in prison for knifing a former girlfriend and trying to kill her. He was known to be controlling and abusive to Mairead and Lisa, and bragged about his previous violence to frighten them. His friends and neighbours spoke of him as if he was a bit of a rogue rather than a dangerous psychopath, and this perspective was visible in mainstream media as Philpott was the subject of attention on the *Jeremy Kyle Show*. His abuse and previous violence was invisible as the media focused on his manipulation of the 'benefits' system, and unorthodox lifestyle, living with two women at the same time. There were a significant number of risk factors that pointed to Philpott being dangerous, not least of which was his appalling violence against women.

Again we see the community, the criminal justice system and the schools excusing an abuser's behaviour even where there is clear danger.

Who commits domestic homicide?

Men who kill their intimate partners, and former intimate partners, are a heterogeneous group. But there are shared high risk behaviours and antecedents which we will discuss. For the purposes of this broad discussion we will split them into three groups: first, those who commit homicide alone; second, those who commit homicide with a self-destructive act (SDA), such as suicide or parasuicide; third, those who commit familicide (for an excellent discussion of the psychology behind familicide we recommend Websdale 2010). We will briefly discuss homicide, and homicide with SDA, just to draw out the basic differences observed in this category for killing.

Homicide with SDA

It is shown that men who commit homicide are different to those who commit homicide with SDA. According to Liem and Roberts (2009) it is more common that a domestic homicide followed by an SDA will be preceded by depressive illness, and threats or attempts to commit suicide. There was evidence in this group of far reaching dependency on the victim and fear of abandonment. Domestic homicide has the highest rate of homicide with SDA, and this is almost exclusively committed by men (Liem and Roberts 2009, Starzomski and Nussbaum 2000). In the homicide with SDA group there is strong evidence to show that the key source of frustration is the perpetrator's inability to live without the victim (Liem and Roberts 2009), and Starzomski and Nussbaum (2000) report that perpetrators of homicide with SDA are unable to cope with severe stress, and may suffer from schizophrenia and morbid jealousy. It is also argued in cases of homicide with SDA that these cases can be viewed as self-destructive, and that the killing of someone who is key to the abuser's identity extends that act of self-destruction (Starzomski and Nussbaum 2000). It has also been found that where there is an attempt to commit suicide in the presence of the victim of abuse, the aggression can be turned outward to the victim, and a homicide results (Liem and Roberts 2009). In many cases suicidal men will stage the homicide to look like a suicide when, actually, the homicide was always planned. Sillito and Salari (2011) report that in homicide with SDA, the children of the victim are more likely to witness the incident rather than be absent or be killed themselves (cited in Chanmugam 2014: 74).

Homicide without SDA

There are those who suggest that men who commit homicide without SDA are acting out a narcissistic rage. Narcissism, or love of self, aims to protect one's self-esteem and when that self-esteem is lowered through rejection, aggression arises to restore the sense of self (Liem and Roberts 2009). These men are likely to have convictions or a history of using violence, which includes domestic violence. This group also includes those who are psychopathic or sociopathic, and thus have more of a sense of entitlement and a lack of empathy or sympathy for anyone else's position but their own. A significant number of abusers score highly for psychopathy and narcissistic personality traits (Scott 2004) and reports suggest this could be between 15 to 30 per cent of abusers (Swogger et al. 2007). Psychopathic offenders are characterised by callousness, a diminished capacity for remorse, impulsive behaviour and superficial charm (Swogger et al. 2007). Huss (2009) states that although psychopathy is found in violent men who also use domestic violence, there was less evidence to suggest a high number who used domestic violence only. Those who are on the psychopathic spectrum may well be good manipulators, they tend to learn how to respond to situations rather than intuitively feeling appropriate responses and this can be revealed by inappropriate emotion (Woodworth et al. 2012). They learn quickly how their behaviour will be received in the context of what they want to achieve from it. This means that they are often able to manipulate police and other professionals, as well as the victim, friends and neighbours. This manipulation is made much easier when dominant discourses give the manipulator many excuses and justifications for their behaviour. For example, a psychopathic man who is controlling and abusing a woman can justify his actions as normal by appealing to 'normal male jealousy' when others are around; he can appeal to male solidarity to mask what are actually dangerous and abnormal behaviours. A clear example of this can be seen in the case of Mick Philpott (Case Study 5) who set fire to his own house in an act of revenge on his intimate partner for leaving him, and killed six of his own children (Dodd 2013). In the run up to the homicides his deeply disturbing control and abuse of two women who were his intimate partners, was consistently justified and excused as normal, but extreme, manly behaviour. He was not challenged by anyone about his bizarre lifestyle and everyone was quick to defend it as merely unorthodox. Woodworth et al. (2012) studied the language use of psychopaths and narcissists and found that they overuse words that relate to themselves, like I and me, which reflects their world view. Psychopathic abusers, or those on the spectrum, may well blame the abuse on the victim, on alcohol or on outsiders, they will rarely take any blame themselves.

Perpetrator treatment

The success or not of perpetrator or batterer programmes remains under debate. It is argued that different programmes will be more or less effective for different groups. However, Scott (2004) suggests that perpetrator programmes are as successful as, if not superior to, substance and alcohol abuse programmes in terms of recidivism. However, it is also suggested these results may be misleading. Experimental studies show little or no effect on re-offending or assault rates (Scott 2004). Scott also reports that re-offending rates for those men who use control and verbal abuse have even lower success rates. Swogger et al. found that there may be higher success rates for those abusers with psychopathy in certain treatment programmes. It is the case that there are many different programmes focusing on different perceived causes for abuse. Jewell and Wormith (2010) looked at completion rates for batterer programmes and found that they suffer from a high level of attrition, between 15 and 58 per cent, and were only associated with a small reduction in violence. Being part of a lower socio-economic group and poor education were linked to non-completion, and it is argued that men with more to lose are more likely to respond to programmes. It was also found that women are more likely to stay with a man who completed a programme (Jewell 2010).

Highest risk behaviour for all groups

The highest risk behaviour for predicting future homicide is a prior history of domestic abuse. Domestic abusers are serial abusers. Contrary to the popular belief that they are responding to the victim's provocative behaviour and losing control, the truth is that they are serial abusers who are *exerting* control. In any risk assessment if there has been prior abuse the risk level rises. They will often use violence to exert control, the most dangerous use weapons, threaten to use weapons and make threats to kill or commit suicide. Sexual assault and stalking in the relationship are high risk behaviours (Campbell et al. 2007).

Highest risk *trigger* for homicide

The biggest *trigger* for an abusive man to commit fatal violence is separation or the threat of separation. Studies of estrangement and homicide have routinely found a very strong correlation (Stark 2007, Polk 1994). It is found from clinical studies that some men are threatened by a loss of control, and will do anything to regain that control. Although there is an increased risk of violence after separation or the announcement of an intention to separate, the relative dangers of staying and going are under-researched. The increased risk for homicide is in the first three months after separation and for up to a year afterwards. Though for some the risk remains long after that period (Campbell et al. 2007). The best assessment of the level of risk posed comes from the victim herself (Richards 2006), where she has recognised or acknowledged the risk. If a woman says she thinks her partner will kill her, or is capable of killing her, this should be taken very seriously. It has been found in studies that women rarely overestimate the danger, they are far more likely to underestimate it. So, where a woman states that she thinks she could be killed this puts her in the high risk category. However, her own *low* risk assessment should not be taken at face value and other risk factors should be considered as usual. Women underestimate for many reasons, and Campbell et al. (2007) suggest that underestimating is sometimes a coping mechanism to deal with the trauma. It is also suggested to be a survival strategy because leaving the relationship would make more real the actual danger the abuser presents.

This tripartite model for high risk, which includes perpetrator history, trigger situation, and victim risk assessment, is a good starting point where a risk assessment tool is not being used. If it is found that there is a history of abuse or violence, especially strangulation or use of a weapon, and the victim has threatened separation and feels her life is in danger or is very frightened, the highest risk score should be considered irrespective of knowledge of the other risk factors. Another key dangerous behaviour is stalking, which Campbell et al. (2007) argue could possibly be even more indicative of homicide than prior abuse. Contrary to media representations of stalkers as being strangers to their object of love or desire, the reality is much more sinister. Stalking is significantly perpetrated by men against women they know, and more often than not against a former partner (Weller et al. 2013). If the stalker was abusive in the prior relationship this is highly predictive of physical assault (Weller et al. 2013). This kind of stalking is also more likely to persist, and is more likely to be resistant to criminal justice intervention, it is also the type of stalking least likely to attract prosecution (Weller et al. 2013). Stalking is an extension of domestic abuse.

It was found in a large US study that 70–90 per cent of attempted IPF included stalking and harassment (Campbell et al. 2007). Stalking was found to have occurred in the majority of femicides in intact marriages where there was no documented history of violence. The most dangerous cluster of stalking behaviours associated with homicide are: following her to work or school; destruction of her property; and leaving threatening messages on an answering machine (Campbell et al. 2007). These behaviours are routinely considered non-serious by police (see Chapter 6). Stark (2013) reports that stalking often occurs *within* the relationship and women can have their movements constantly watched, be followed from room to room, and have their communications surveilled. Despite worrying evidence that intimate partners and former intimate partners present the most risk, studies have shown that police and the public perceive the danger to be much lower than it really is. They perceive more danger when there is no prior intimate relationship although the reverse is actually more accurate (Scott et al. 2010; Scott and Sheridan 2011 cited in Weller et al. 2013).

Other factors which designate highest risk for homicide are: access to a gun (USA), threats to kill or threats with a weapon, non-fatal strangulation and suicide threats (Campbell et al. 2007). Particularly dangerous men are those who beat pregnant women and force sex on them (Campbell et al. 2007). Non-fatal strangulation has been shown in some studies to increase the risk sevenfold for a homicide (Campbell et al. 2007). Pregnancy increases the risk of homicide significantly and is the leading cause of maternal mortality (Campbell et al. 2007). Pregnant and newly pregnant women are two to three times more at risk for homicide. African American women and young women are at the greatest risk of pregnancy related homicide. Factors which are high risk in conjunction with coercion and control are, a stepchild in the home, and unemployment.

There are now risk assessment tools in routine use by multiple agencies to assess the risk for homicide. In the UK we primarily use the DASH (domestic abuse, sexual and honour based violence) and SPECCS+ models. These tools have brought together many of the known high risk behaviours and put them in the form of questions. The victim is scored as high, medium or standard risk depending on the number of risks a victim can confirm, or that have been witnessed, as present. High risk victims will most often be referred on for specialist help, support or safety planning. We will now go through some of the high risk characteristics used to predict dangerousness or risk for homicide or serious assault in commonly used risk assessment tools:

1. Previous domestic abuse
2. The woman is frightened that she is in serious danger
3. Separation or the threat of separation
4. Sexual assault
5. Threats to use, or use of, a weapon
6. Threats to kill her or her children
7. Threats to commit suicide
8. Violence, especially escalation in seriousness or frequency
9. Pregnancy (especially violence)
10. Stepchildren in the home
11. Stalking or harassment
12. Strangulation, simulated or real
13. Threats to kill loved ones or pets
14. Arguments over child contact

Abusers in the system

Another problem which ought to be considered is the number of police officers and professionals who are abusers themselves and how this may affect their response to domestic abuse. Although there have been relatively few studies which estimate the number of officers who are abusive, the prevalence in American studies suggests a rate of around 40 per cent. This is higher than the rate for the military (32 per cent) or the general population at 10 per cent (Lonsway 2006). Lonsway (2006) suggests that these findings could be rather conservative given that they relied on self-reporting. From our research we found that police and paramedics were particularly reluctant to accept that their colleagues could be abusers (see Chapter 6). We also found from our research that many police officers were victims of domestic abuse. We did not find that police victims of domestic abuse were any more satisfied with the police's response than any other group. It was considered by many police officers that victims might not be the best officers to handle domestic abuse calls. This related to the general perception that victims would not be objective. One officer in particular expressed the view that he would screen domestic abuse victims out of specialist domestic abuse teams, but would not screen for abusers in the teams (see Chapter 6).

Responding to victims of domestic abuse and homicide

Many of our professional interviewees were unhappy with having to deal with domestic abuse, some claimed it was trivial and frustrating and some considered it outside their professional skill set. Again, the biggest problems are blamed on the victims or seen to be because of them. Professionals recognised the sensitive nature of the abuse and control and didn't feel comfortable talking to victims. They felt they might upset them, or say the wrong thing, or make a decision which put the victim in more danger. This suggested that the professionals did not feel confident that they knew how to properly respond, and this is one of the reasons multi-agency training can be so beneficial. A clearer picture of the whole system may give individual professionals the confidence and knowledge to proceed. Szilassy et al. found, in a study of domestic violence and child protection, that interagency and interprofessional training can 'promote an understanding of the roles and responsibilities of professionals working in different organizations ... and increase the ability of professionals to recognize and identify signs of domestic violence and the particular power dynamics associated with it' (2014: 1383). More importantly, Szilassy et al. found that professionals were more likely to take action in talking to victims and perpetrators and referring on after they had completed interagency training. The professionals we spoke with had little understanding of the policies and resources of other organisations and, along with information being kept in silos much of the time, this created a lack of confidence in dealing with domestic abuse and a powerful reluctance to get involved. It is easier to blame the victim than request training. Most police officers we spoke with absolutely declared that they did not need or want training in domestic abuse responding (see Chapter 6).

This attitude is perpetuated in discourses of female victims. The activism of second wave feminists has given high profile publicity since the 1970s to violence against women, and this has highlighted the appalling abuse of women in many different contexts the world over, through homicide, trafficking, rape and sexual assault, pornography, prostitution and domestic abuse to name but a few. From our research we found that the victims of domestic abuse are popularly considered to be psychologically damaged, to the point that they cannot be spoken to as if they were normal human subjects. Certainly, the kind of violence and abuse we are talking about causes trauma, and very often serious trauma, but this should not frighten people away from talking to women who are victims. Professionals need to be confident that they have enough knowledge of the system that they can give advice and deal with the emotion and repercussions. It is suggested that professionals need to build a rapport with someone to conduct any kind of interview or conversation where sensitive information is to be given. Fogarty et al. (2013) discuss rapport building with child victims of sexual abuse and say that it is an important priority, especially where children are expected to talk about potentially embarrassing subjects. Rapport building is also an integral part of the PEACE framework for investigative interviewing, and that will include the interviewing of criminals who may not be considered as fragile as vulnerable victims. It seems that professionals from all agencies do not feel they are able to have a rapport with domestic abuse victims.

The professional has a job to do, and that can only be done with confidence if the professional knows exactly how to help the individual in need. The backlash against victims of domestic abuse may, in some part, be a product of the way she makes the professional feel powerless. Fogarty et al. suggest that rapport building is often seen as an intuitive thing, and just means a requirement to make the other person feel comfortable enough to give sensitive and difficult information (2013: 397). The professionals we spoke with talked about not feeing skilled enough to take on such a role. Certainly, building a rapport can be a complex task, but it can also be achieved through shared goals and a shared understanding of the situation. It is even suggested that there should be shared physical emotion. Many ways are suggested to achieve rapport; like interactional synchrony, which can mean mimicking the other person's posture and body language (Fogarty et al. 2013), matching their rate of speech and even breathing, and making sure they know you are listening by repeating things they say and approving of them. For example, nodding your head or saying something like, 'fantastic, I agree' or 'you are so right'. This can create a feeling of empathy. Fogarty et al. also suggest that rapport should not be judged by absolute presence or absence, they suggest that different levels of rapport can be present at different points in a conversation (2013: 397)

Lindhorst et al. (2008) suggest that there must be trust between the professional and the victim, or she will not talk about abuse. They also note that the benefits and risks of disclosure need to be clear to her (Lindhorst et al. 2008). She is often chronically fearful and disclosure is a potentially dangerous action for her. She may fear her disclosure will be put into writing and that her abuser may see it one day. This kind of thing happens all the time. A woman who disclosed her abuse to an organisation later found they had summarised the interview in writing and posted it back to her home address for her information. Ridiculous and clumsy practices like this are dangerous, and victims showed little faith that anyone truly understood their fear, at least enough for them to feel comfortable disclosing abuse and speaking out against the abuser. Professionals who appear disinterested or uncaring are perceived as untrustworthy (Lindhorst et al. 2008), with no trust there is no rapport, and so the victim will not disclose, she may lie, she may be rude, she may be difficult, in order to get rid of that person she does not trust.

So trust is crucial. It may be that professionals feel uncomfortable talking with victims because they don't trust the system themselves, and rapport under those circumstances is difficult to achieve. There must be honesty about the limits of the level of confidentiality that can be achieved, confidentiality is a deterrent to disclosure (Lindhorst et al. 2008). Professionals should be prepared to tell her what the benefits of disclosure, or any action a professional wants or advises her to take, are. If professionals don't know what the benefits are, they should find out. Following an organisational agenda without knowing the benefit to the victim, and making her believe there are benefits makes the interview disingenuous and dangerous for her. She is capable of making decisions about her safety given the truth and the support to follow available paths. Is prosecution going to help her? Professionals should be prepared to tell her how it will help, and what happens if the prosecution fails.

It is also argued that a clear care pathway creates confidence for practitioners. Care pathways are more commonplace in a health-care setting where such processes are the norm. Co-ordinated Action Against Domestic Abuse (CAADA) has produced comprehensive advice for healthcare practitioners with a clear care pathway identified, which includes a process pathway:

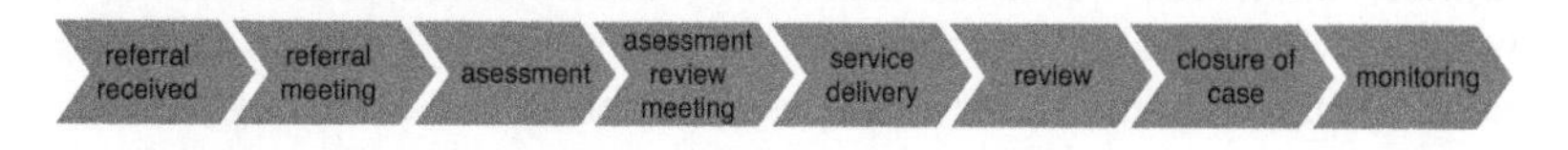

Rigorous evidence gathering, a caring and supportive interview and a clear pathway for the victim will make an interview with the victim a professional and beneficial interaction (Szilassy et al. 2014, Othman et al. 2014, Lindhorst et al. 2008). Officers do not need special training in being supportive, they need to resist the discursive truths that construct the victim as a problem. Approach her as a victim of abuse who needs to know what her options are. Believe her, be honest with her, be supportive of her, and address the abuser's behaviour (Szilassy et al. 2014, Othman et al. 2014, Hester 2013a, Lindhorst et al. 2008, Stark 2007).

Lindhorst et al. (2008) researched screening for domestic abuse in a welfare setting and found the following the most successful in encouraging disclosure:

1. Build rapport through active listening and empathetic reflection.
2. Ensure that any disclosure of abuse is confidential.
3. Explain the reasons why disclosure would be beneficial.
4. Ask clients directly about abuse.
5. Define abuse broadly, with physical, sexual, and emotional components.
6. Use both open-ended probes and behaviourally anchored questions.
7. Avoid questions that force a woman to identify with a stigmatised status.
8. Provide multiple opportunities for disclosure within interviews and over time. Lindhorst et al. (2008: 9)

If women are asked if they are victims of abuse they may well deny it for many reasons; it is better to talk about patterns of behaviour, which include things like sexual assault and harassment, rather than focusing on violence (Lindhorst et al. 2008). Some professionals have expressed a concern that when women deny abuse it may be because they are offended, but research has shown that women are more likely to disclose where repeated enquiries are made and they feel that domestic abuse is part of the organisational agenda, and may well disclose in the future if not at that particular meeting. Women actually find it acceptable to be asked about abuse, and it is suggested they prefer it when healthcare professionals in particular take the initiative (Bradbury-Jones and Taylor 2013).

Asking open-ended questions about threat and safety, and behaviourally anchored questions about the abuse is recommended. The woman will probably not agree to anything which includes labelling her a 'battered woman', for example. Othman et al. (2014) suggest that barriers to disclosing abuse will be complex and include shame, loyalty and gender identity, they also note that in their sample of Malaysian women there was intense fear of the abuser, coupled with a complex gratitude for his allowing her to have food and a home (2014: 1504). Victims of domestic abuse are not weak and without agency, they negotiate their lives with a dangerous abuser on a daily basis, they can be spoken to with truth, respect and a caring attitude. Far from weakness Othman et al. note exceptionally high levels of endurance and tolerance in abused women (2014: 1505).

As a final comment on talking with female victims of abuse it is interesting to note that one of the key barriers to women reporting or even disclosing abuse is the fear they will be forced to leave the relationship or pursue a prosecution (Orthman et al. 2014); the two things complained about by professionals in criminal justice especially. These two things make her so afraid she would rather continue suffering the abuse until she sees a way out she trusts.

In conclusion, domestic abuse and homicide is a serious and endemic problem which victimises women far more than men. The dominant discourses which construct the abuse, the victim, and the perpetrator have a significant influence in structuring what we know about domestic abuse or IPA. However, these understandings are limited and negatively impact on responses to the abuse by professionals, and on safety planning for victims.

Case Study 6: Harriet

Harriet managed to leave her abusive partner after years of violence and control. He had assaulted her by strangulation twice, and she had lost consciousness on one occasion. Her partner Michael moved in with another woman, but still kept contact with Harriet as they shared children (now adults). Michael still called regularly, sometimes he followed Harriet and questioned her about her movements. He got angry and continued to hit Harriet. She couldn't have a relationship with anyone because she feared Michael would kill her. Harriet called the police recently because Michael had let himself into her house. He was warned about his behaviour. Then Harriet called the police because he stole her mobile phone. He returned it when the police asked. Harriet again called police because she thought there was a prowler. Police found no one.

What would you do with Harriet's case?

What actually happened: Harriet is now dead, strangled by Michael.

5
Police and Paramedics: Policy and Practice

Policy and practice

Police and paramedics are probably the most regular responders to calls for *immediate* help from victims of domestic abuse. We acknowledge that disclosing abuse is equally likely to occur in other settings than an emergency, but we are now going to focus on police and paramedics and calls for immediate assistance. Very often calls for immediate assistance may be about injury, or harassment, or anti-social behaviour, or assault and may not be made by the victim. The main tasks may well be in crisis management and that is very different to considered safety planning. We have found that the processes in place for first responders, whether they be paramedics or police, are often inconsistent with the expectations of those who have an interest in safety planning for victims of abuse. It seems that two things are clear which may not be immediately obvious: first, victims often recognise that first responders can only manage the immediate threat and they do not always expect to start a long term safety plan after a 999 call – victims of domestic abuse are using the system largely in the way it has been designed to be used; second, the attitude of officers or paramedics is far more important to victims than any ongoing safety planning they can offer *at that time*. Victims are not always convinced that police officers or paramedics can keep them safe. Confidence and trust in the system can be furthered by professionals believing the victim and recognising she is scared and has a safety strategy.

There is a problem with the status of domestic abuse, which constructs it as different to other calls for help. It seems that domestic abuse is not the final responsibility of any service in particular; professionals often feel they are dealing with something outside their formal remit or area of expertise. Paramedics often see it as a police responsibility, and police describe it as social work. There is a collective lack of responsibility for the problem of domestic abuse. Because our emergency services are geared up to deal with 'incidents' that fall into specific areas of expertise, they are not always equipped to provide ongoing support, or to respond to an abstractedly connected series of incidents, which may or may not fall within their area of expertise.

Domestic abuse first needs to be identified. Health care professionals, specifically those who respond in an emergency medical care role, are ideally placed to uncover potential domestic abuse or violence. Emergency medical services (EMS) personnel are often received into the home environment with a much lower level of suspicion than the police or social services. However, although access to the home is not usually an issue, as it may be for the police, recognising and correctly responding to IPA remains problematic. Arguably, specific training and education are the best way forward in giving professionals the skills to recognise and identify abuse. Despite the popular rhetoric, abuse is not always self-evident, and many professionals don't understand the basic psychology or dynamics, as is evidenced by their frustration with victims who will neither support prosecutions nor leave abusive men.

Responding to a call for help is also fraught with other difficulties, it is a potentially dangerous situation for professional and victim, quite often alcohol, high emotion and violence are involved. For this reason, and given the complexities of the context, professionals may enter 'domestic' incidents with some trepidation. Sometimes they find themselves physically threatened, sometimes the victim will be uncooperative, or intoxicated or suffering with a mental health disturbance. Many things may be happening where the professional feels caught in the middle, powerless, concerned and confused. It may be difficult to identify criminal behaviour or who the offender is, or if there are injuries and to whom. But unprofessional, inappropriate or insensitive management of such situations may increase the likelihood of further abuse, or of retaliation against the woman. Also, this visit may be the one chance that anyone gets to intervene. If the woman receives a poor service she may not accept the help offered at the time or ever call for help again.

From a police perspective it is suggested to us that it is sometimes difficult to identify who the offender is. In this context the offender will not necessarily be the person who has been perpetrating abuse for a protracted period. The offender in an 'incident', which is the context for the police, will be, for example, the person who has committed the assault *at that time* or a criminal damage. This may well be the victim of

- Traumatic injuries arising as a direct result of assault
- Stress related conditions, including: irritable bowel syndrome, backache, headaches, depression, anxiety, post-traumatic stress disorder, self harm and suicide
- Increased incidence of sexually transmitted infections and unplanned pregnancy, often resulting in termination or low birthweight babies

Figure 5.1 Examples of the clinical consequences of domestic violence

abuse. Often, the victim will be manipulated by the abuser into a situation where she is breaking the law and appears to be the provoking party. Certainly, police report that in attending 'domestics' they seek to calm the situation, identify offences and offenders, and make sure everyone is safe. This works for standard relationships, but can be a more problematic response for domestic abuse. The situation is equally difficult for paramedics. Identifying a woman who is suffering, or who has suffered, abuse at the hands of a partner or family member can be extremely difficult as the clinical consequences of IPA can manifest themselves in many ways (Taket et al. 2003).

For various and deeply complex reasons, the woman may feel protective towards the abuser, or may pretend she does; she may be afraid to disclose the true details of the incident or injury since the outcome she desires may not be as simple as just removing the abuser, upon whom she may be financially or emotionally reliant. This reluctance to disclose or a blatant covering-up of the true events can make it difficult or even impossible for the EMS personnel to obtain a logical or honest history upon which to base a diagnosis, issue advice or instigate a treatment regime.

Information and data

Documentation of the incident is also difficult and different attending organisations will record responses separately from each other, and even separately from other departments within the same organisation. It appears that sharing information between emergency services and general practitioners (GPs), for example, is not always done, and GPs have no automatic access to hospital data, and vice versa. In the case of the police, an incident log contains certain information, but this is not the same information as in a risk assessment, which is recorded and kept separately, or in a history and markers recorded against the victim, perpetrator or the address. All this information is often kept in different places, accessed by different people and not integrated into a chronology for future visits by first responders.

In some control rooms call handlers will have to go to multiple databases to access information recorded about previous calls, but this is almost impossible to achieve during the crucial minutes of a 999 call, and in the stress of multiple calls for service. Often, information from DASH risk assessments or HITS screening is not accessible at all. In this respect the attending emergency personnel will have to respond only to what they see at that 'incident', without a supporting history. Their documentation may then enter the system, isolated from other information. Certainly, paramedic and police records on an incident do not meet. This makes an informed risk assessment and safety plan very difficult to achieve. For example, it is general ambulance service procedure to complete a document that will act as a permanent record of the incident. This record will provide details relating to the previous and present medical history of the patient (as told to the paramedic by the individual at the time) and any subsequent clinical management delivered. This document, commonly referred to in UK ambulance services as a Patient Clinical Record or a Patient Report Form (PCR/PRF), not only represents a paper record, which will enable the patient's clinical information to be quickly and easily shared with other necessary medical services, but it is also a legal record of the history of the incident and of any treatment given.

Accurate and timely reporting of events using appropriate official documentation is essential. The PCR/PRF, or other such clinical records, will be used as a reference point both inside and outside the hospital environment and can, in effect, be used to evidence the events leading up to, during and following an event/incident. It is common practice for hospitals, solicitors and police services to request copies of these records for use in situations where a claim for compensation may arise due to negligence, or for use in either the prosecution or the defence (Caroline 2008) of a criminal case in a court of law. But, and for our purposes more importantly, these records are not available to paramedics who are attending a call for help. They do not have any immediate access to previous PCRs and HITS assessments. Similarly in many cases, police officers do not have access to previous DASH risk assessments. This is particularly concerning because those women who are in the most danger are usually repeat victims, who need their risk assessed on the basis of a history of a course of conduct by the abuser. Domestic abuse is not made up of isolated incidents, and risk cannot be assessed on this basis. The police and paramedics are attending 'single isolated incidents' and assessing risk based on whatever information they may be able to get from the victim and the situation. There may be some information available on databases, and some police services have domestic abuse databases where they may record information about previous calls. Police databases can give important information but, like paramedic record keeping, this needs to be accurate and complete using the official documents. It is important that in all situations where an emergency response is required, and especially those where a potential criminal or safeguarding issue arises, that professional responders appreciate the absolute importance of recording the behaviour and, whenever reasonably practicable, adopt the habit of transcribing any brief verbal account provided by individuals at the scene (this may necessitate an additional page as the PCR/PRF document has very limited available space). Whenever possible, recording the accounts of key individuals in the language used is vitally important, as this information might be referred to as evidence in a court of law in the future. Certainly, good early evidence collection may help in a prosecution that may not have the explicit help of the victim.

Best practice is that police officers are trained in using DASH risk assessment forms. But that training is not consistent across the country. Some services only use computer-based packages for training, which require an individual to click through screens to show they have read the content. Police officers readily admit that in many cases they frequently do not read the pages. This means many officers are receiving little training in responding to domestic abuse and how to effectively assess risk, except that which they receive from the stories of experienced colleagues. Some police services are much better than others in this respect and regular face to face training and exposure to specialists is provided. EMS staff across the UK currently receive regular programmes of continuing professional education (CPD), some of which is provided through the employing organisation and will be informed by statutory and mandatory government guidance. Education relating to wider safeguarding issues is currently delivered throughout all UK ambulance services, and information and guidance relating to child abuse and the abuse of adults is well represented. IPA and domestic abuse however, is still quite poorly addressed and receives little time when compared to educational preparation in relation to the management of the abuse of children or other vulnerable adult groups, such as those requiring specific consideration in relation to mental capacity or those who are vulnerable through age. All UK EMS organisations have access to a dedicated safeguarding lead who is responsible for ensuring that staff can access appropriate programmes of education in relation to safeguarding issues, but there exists a wide diversity between organisations as to how and in what measure this information and knowledge is disseminated to staff.

Having the ability to sympathise and understand the position in which victims can often find themselves will go some way to help ensure that EMS and police personnel can offer appropriate support and advice. This sympathy and understanding will, in some measure, help the victim to attempt to maintain control, manage and hopefully improve their situation. But to make any significant impact, professionals need to have the ability to recognise abuse and utilise appropriate support services in order to support the abused woman in affecting any permanent change in her situation. Many officers and paramedics express frustration with victims who do not make their job easier; especially those who would not cooperate with a prosecution, or would not speak against the abuser. Sometimes victims actively appear to side with the abuser against a paramedic or police officer. This reduces the amount of sympathy felt by professionals, but does not reduce the risk posed to the victim.

In 2011, a review of domestic abuse policies in England and Wales (Matczak et al. 2011) was undertaken, and its conclusion stated that the 'one size fits all' approach for all agencies was not suitable as 'different institutions speak different languages'. It is therefore essential to consider, when developing an education package or training plan suitable for EMS or other agencies, that although consistency within the overall objective is important, a multi-disciplinary approach should be adopted which recognises and values the diversity and differing priorities of the agencies involved. Often, the priorities of an organisation can be overlooked in stressing the victim's agenda. Different agencies have different tools, skills and powers to deal with various aspects of domestic abuse. There is no one agency that can deal with domestic abuse alone, despite the heavy responsibility placed upon police officers.

In relation to the involvement of the police service, there are currently strong recommendations to reduce the reliance upon the criminal justice system to address domestic abuse. Criminal law is observed to be more concerned with punishing the abuser than offering assistance or support to the abused. Although many people would argue that criminal interventions are more often necessary than not, further solutions in relation to the prevention of abuse and the support of victims are needed (Matczak et al. 2011). There is a conspicuous absence of any policy or procedure which concentrates on addressing the behaviour, issues or motivations of the perpetrator. It is all too common to read about how each policy intends to address reducing the risk for the victim, without acknowledging the actual cause of that risk, the abuser. In fact, when victims do not cooperate they are often seen as the problem. Such is the prevalence of this attitude that abusers can very often manipulate police and others into believing that it is they who are suffering from unfair criticism by the victim. Sometimes professionals will side with the abuser, even designating them victim status. This is a pattern of control frequently used by many abusers.

The Welsh Government's (WG) Violence Against Women and Domestic Abuse draft budget for 2011/2012 amounted to approximately £4.4 million, and the Social Justice Minister launched the *Right to be Safe – Violence Against Women* strategy in March of 2012 as a pledge to use this funding to tackle the issues of domestic abuse. The six-year integrated strategy addresses all forms of violence against women in Wales, including rape and sexual assault, domestic abuse, honour based violence, female genital mutilation and forced marriage.[1] The strategy will work alongside and in partnership with the UK government strategy,[2] which in itself contains a range of actions for non-devolved bodies and criminal justice measures that will apply across England and Wales.

Of course, domestic abuse is not restricted to England and Wales, and medical services all over the world are facing similar issues. According to a report from the Department of Health and Human Services[3] in the United States of America, the cost of intimate partner rape, physical assault, and stalking in 2003 exceeded $5.8 billion, nearly $4.1 billion of which was absorbed by the victims requiring access to medical and mental health services, and this figure has the potential to rise year upon year. The largest component of IPV-related costs in the USA is reported to be directly attributable to the provision of health care, which accounts for more than two-thirds of the total cost. The individual states within America are responding by developing strategies to address the issues related to the growing demands placed upon the medical services. The American College of Emergency Physicians[4] believes that

> training in the evaluation and management of victims of domestic violence should be incorporated into the initial and continuing education of EMS personnel [and they continue by suggesting that] this training should include the recognition of victims and their injuries, an understanding of the patterns of abuse and how this affects care, scene safety, preservation of evidence, and documentation requirements.

Following a collaboration between the New Mexico Department of Health, the EMS Bureau, the Community Health Services Division, the EMS Academy and the University of New Mexico's Department of Emergency Medicine, an EMS response manual was developed, the aim of which is to equip and train New Mexico EMS personnel with the necessary tools to properly identify, treat and refer patients who are victims of domestic violence.

EMS personnel training and education in England and Wales

Utilising the diverse range of policy and procedural guidance currently available in Wales the Welsh Ambulance Services NHS Trust (WAST) developed a programme of education and training aimed specifically at preparing EMS personnel to recognise and react appropriately to signs of domestic abuse.[5] The Welsh Government Violence Against Women and Domestic Abuse Implementation Plan[6] aimed to publish a national training strategy in 2011–2012 and, in line with current guidance, WAST put policies in place to support EMS staff in managing domestic abuse both in the field[7] and in the workplace. WAST was establishing itself as a leader in the field of preparing EMS personnel to recognise and appropriately respond to situations involving potential domestic abuse, and to enable personnel to recognise the importance of the role they have to offer in the provision of support to women who find themselves in these extremely complex and dangerous situations.

The Central and Northwest London NHS Foundation and the Outer and North East London NHS, for example, have both produced detailed policy and procedural guidance for use by its personnel across the wider NHS. North East London and the City produced a guide to support and enable victims of domestic abuse to contact appropriate support services, the *Contacting Domestic Violence Support Services in Outer North East London* guide card was supported by the NHS and by local councils in Outer North East London in an effort to address the issues.

Barking and Dagenham NHS are another prime example of the many organisations reacting to the need to implement guidance for personnel to enable domestic abuse to be identified and appropriately responded to.[8] The South East Coast ambulance service (SECAmb) stated in their 2010 report[9] that one of their key objectives was to

> increase awareness amongst SECAmb clinical staff around issues relating to managing the clinical needs, risks and making appropriate service provision for women and children [including boys] at risk of violence, but who have historically been less able to disclose abuse.

The reference contained in the above is particularly poignant as this objective refers to individuals who have 'historically been less able to disclose abuse', this is interesting as it identifies closely with the concept of a means of enabling victims through facilitating a discussion where disclosure is easier. A methodology which might assist in this notion was outlined in the UK by the Department of Health in 2004 and is called the routine enquiry (RE).

Routine enquiry

The Department of Health first introduced the concept of RE in 2004. It was seen as a more suitable approach to accessing a domestic abuse history from women than the method traditionally used, which was screening. Screening tended to follow a standard set of questions or apply a test, neither of which differed between the many situations where it was employed. RE is perceived as being a more suitable approach for domestic abuse as the procedures used by the differing health care providers, in wide and varied situations, will fluctuate greatly, 'questions are asked routinely in certain settings, or if indicators of abuse arise' (Taket et al. 2003).[10] Yet Sullivan and Websdale (2006) report that fewer than ten per cent of primary care physicians in their study routinely screened for domestic abuse. And in the case of men, screening is hardly ever done in a healthcare setting.

In the United Kingdom, over 90 per cent of the population will come into contact with the primary healthcare services within five years (Taket et al. 2003). Although those services will not necessarily be the emergency services, the opportunity has been recognised for making a routine enquiry. In situations where a clinical history is routinely recorded, initiating conversations relating to a woman's medical as well as domestic situation is much easier if the woman is already expecting to answer a variety of questions. EMS personnel are accustomed to asking patients these types of questions as part of both primary and secondary clinical assessments referred to as 'surveys'. Primary and secondary surveys can occur in many and varied situations. A primary survey is a set of questions, or more commonly a set of observations (pulse, respiration and so on), which are swiftly recorded by the attending EMS staff to establish if any life threatening medical conditions exist. If the result of the primary survey is that no life threatening conditions exist, then a secondary survey is usually undertaken, which is a slower and wider assessment of the patient. Adding a routine enquiry to this common history gathering procedure (secondary survey) would mean that some of the questions posed could be specifically designed to enable victims of domestic abuse to feel comfortable enough to disclose personal and intimate details of their domestic situation. The secondary survey can be undertaken as part of a routine and more supportive conversation or discussion with the patient. The Central and North West London Foundation NHS Trust (CNWL) recommends that all service users should be asked about their experience of abuse at the hands of a partner or family member,[11] and ambulance personnel are provided with training and education to assist them in early recognition of situations where there exists a potential for domestic abuse. EMS staff are encouraged to routinely inquire whenever there is a situation that lends itself to tactful and careful questioning which would be accepted as part of the 'business as usual' clinical history recording process.

In the WAST, EMS staff receive an introductory three-hour session relating specifically to domestic abuse. The session, delivered across Wales, includes a slide show presentation, group discussion and consolidation quiz. To assist staff in absorbing what can be a complex and diverse topic, and to assist in the process of appropriate scene management, ambulance services across the UK are using various mnemonics to represent a set of reminders or structured questions, formulated to act as an aide memoire to EMS staff. In CNWL the mnemonic RADAR is used to prompt personnel to follow guidelines (Figure 5.2)

Following significant changes in the provision of Health Services in Wales, the WAST discusses in its 'Working Together for Success' programme,[12] that the future delivery of pre-hospital care within Wales will be to treat more patients at home to reduce inappropriate hospital admissions, therefore a procedure for offering advice to possible victims of domestic abuse has been developed for patients who are not transported to hospital. RE is a concept most readily associated with the health services, for the reasons outlined. It is not something that police officers are encouraged to do. It may be more difficult for police officers to ask such questions, especially as they could be accused of seeking to

R – Routine Enquiry
A – Ask direct questions
D – Document findings accurately
A – Assess service users safety
R – Resources: give service users information on resources available and Respect their choices

Figure 5.2 RADARR Tool

criminalise someone where there had been no complaint. Women rarely approach police for general domestic abuse advice. Police are generally used to try and manage immediate danger when the complainant is the victim (Hester 2013a). Families of victims are known to seek police advice and support when concerned about safety but police are often reluctant to get involved unless the victim has made a direct complaint, or an incident is ongoing. Training for police in domestic abuse awareness and risk assessment should be fairly uniform, but, as noted, the way officers are trained is quite different depending on which police service they work for. Some services have more support than others. A recent HMIC (2014) report on domestic abuse responses across the country by police identified good and bad areas of practice, but the overall conclusion was that service was poor and that only eight out of the 43 services were providing a good service. In England, police and other services use the DASH risk assessment tool. This is a set of questions representing high risk behaviours which raise the level of danger for the woman. The set of questions forms the basis for a risk assessment interview. This interview is described as time consuming by many frontline and senior officers and there have been moves by some police services to reduce the time it takes to complete the interview by removing some of the questions, or to reduce the number of interviews which take place, or both. Training in how to perform a risk assessment interview using a DASH form is also a bit of a, so-called, postcode lottery. Officers in many areas told us that they didn't realise the importance of the questions, or of the order in which they were asked. Many officers had not had any training at all.

It is the case that a proper risk assessment will take time because it is a course of conduct that is being assessed not a single incident. However, good training will alert officers to the most high risk behaviours and a risk assessment could be much more efficient. A DASH assessment is not a RE and is advised in all cases categorised as domestic. Officers complain that some domestic incident calls do not warrant any kind of risk assessment and the blanket approach is not appropriate. The DASH form is quite comprehensive and is an excellent tool for a risk assessment interview, but lack of training in how to use it and why it is being used, is undermining its utility in safety planning. Where an officer can confidently score someone as high risk, there may be a stronger care pathway. If risk is not high, then the response is less clear. Some places have had so many high risk cases that they are now placing them in a hierarchy of 'high risk, and very high risk'. There is also some confusion about what high risk means. In some cases it is assumed to be that the abuser presents a high risk for homicide due to his behaviours so the victim needs a safety plan and enhanced help, but it is also written into some policies that it is the time scale during which the homicide might occur which will designate the risk level. For example, a victim would only be designated high risk if the homicide is predicted to occur in the next 24 hours. This seems to be an impossible assessment to make and will not help any but those victims where a specific and imminent threat has been made. Why this type of threat needs a DASH risk assessment to be revealed is not clear, one would assume that any threat to kill in the next 24 hours would be taken seriously in any circumstances. It is also not helpful that a multi agency risk assessment conference (MARAC) or other referral may not happen in many cases for at least 48 hours.

In Wales the HITS tool (also referred to as the DA1) has been developed by Welsh hospital emergency departments and subsequently introduced to establish the RE phase. The HITS tool assists personnel in structuring appropriate questions to facilitate a discussion relating to potential domestic abuse.[13] Universal screening for domestic abuse is supported as being best practice if all of the following criteria apply:[14]

- The patient/service user is 16 years of age or over
- The patient/service user is alone
- It is safe to do so
- The patient/service user is not critically injured/ill

It is advised that this method of RE is undertaken as part of the general practice of history taking, which would form a usual component of what is called the secondary survey (the primary survey being that which will establish the presence or absence of any life threatening illness or injury). The HITS should be utilised wherever and whenever it is identified as being appropriate. Permission will first be gained from the individual before asking any of the questions to establish that they are comfortable in consenting to participate in the RE. Some GPs use a screening tool in RE called HARK. The HARK acronym reflects four questions, which are:

Humiliation: within the last year, have you been humiliated or emotionally abused in other ways by your partner or your ex-partner?
Afraid: within the last year, have you been afraid of your partner or ex-partner?
Rape: within the last year, have you been raped or forced to have any kind of sexual activity by your partner or ex-partner?

Kick: within the last year, have you been kicked, hit, slapped or otherwise physically hurt by your partner or ex-partner? (Sohal et al. 2012)

The HITS tool is printed onto a pocket sized card and distributed to all EMS personnel in Wales following attendance at a mandatory training and education session (Figure 5.3). The pocket card acts as an aide memoire and provides guidance to staff who need to broach sensitive subjects, such as possible or suspected domestic abuse. Any information disclosed by the individual can then easily be recorded onto the PCR/PRF document by the EMS personnel.

HITS Questionnaire	**Use only when person is alone**	**Score 0**	**Score 1**
Hurt	Does your partner or anyone else at home physically hurt you?	No	Yes
Insult	Does your partner or anyone else at home insult, talk down to you or control you?	No	Yes
Threaten	Do you feel threatened in your current relationship?	No	Yes
Shout / Safe	Does your partner, ex-partner or anyone else at home shout or swear at you so that you feel unsafe?	No	Yes
Total Score	Can be recorded on PCR as: H I T S	Score of 1 or more is highly suggestive of abuse occurring	

Figure 5.3a HITS tool, aide memoire (front of pocket card)

What can be asked? (An example of how the topic can be introduced)

Latest figures indicate that 1 in 4 women and 1 in 7 men experience domestic abuse. By way of ensuring that victims of abuse are offered appropriate support and protection, WAST in conjunction with other parts of the NHS in Wales is now routinely asking patients / service users whether they are affected by domestic abuse

I am therefore going to ask you some questions which are not intended to cause any offence

Figure 5.3b continued

Indirect

1. Is everything alright at home?
2. Is your partner supportive and caring?
3. Will you get plenty of support at home after calling us today

Direct

1. Do you ever feel frightened of your partner or anyone else at home?
2. Have you been hit, kicked, punched or otherwise hurt by someone within the past year?
3. Do you feel safe in your current relationship now?
4. Is there a partner from a previous relationship who is making you feel unsafe now?

Figure 5.3b HITS tool, aide memoire (reverse of pocket card)

Once domestic abuse is recognised, what happens next?

It is important to note that whether the patient travels to the hospital or not, it is only after consent has been gained from the patient that any referral to other services can be made on their behalf, but the feeling of it 'not being our business' is all too familiar. This is the same for police services, victims of domestic abuse must consent to be referred on to specialist services, though MARACs can be held without the victim knowing. It is usual practice for any victim to be referred to a MARAC after being assessed as high risk with the DASH tool. There is space on the DASH form for victims to agree or not to being referred to a specialist domestic abuse support agency. If this is not ticked, or the officer forgets to ask, then no referral can be made.

Where the patient provides consent to be transported to an emergency department (ED) for further clinical treatment or assessment, the information that was gained from the routine enquiry (HITS assessment) will be presented to the hospital staff as part of the PCR/PRF history record. If the HITS score is recorded on the PCR/PRF as being positive (score above 1), the patient should now be offered a DA2 assessment.

The DA2 is a continuation of the HITS Assessment (DA1) Routine Enquiry, and this section is completed when there has been a disclosure of abuse or it has been identified that ambulance staff have recognised a positive HITS score (DA1) or have given a help and support card. The DA2 will be undertaken by hospital or associated staff who have received specific and specialised training, and this will hopefully uncover any further risks that the victim may be subject to. Again, it is important to note that only after consent has been gained from the individual can any referral to other services be made. If the patient does not travel to the ED, they will be provided with an advice card. This card contains the telephone number of NHS Direct Wales or English equivalent. The victim is encouraged to contact this number and to request a further DA2 assessment at a time most convenient to them.

In November 2010 policy and guidance on patients and service users who are experiencing domestic abuse was introduced into the WAST. On 1 November 2011 a 'snapshot' audit of the compliance of EMS was undertaken. The audit was a retrospective snapshot audit looking at a convenience sample of PCRs relating to calls attended during January 2011.[15] The audit concluded:

> As there was no reference to a HITS assessment in 98.4% (2438/2478) of PCRs it was concluded that the Routine Enquiry was not considered for these patients. It is apparent that the introduction of Routine Enquiry into WAST has not been a success.

However, there will be further auditing completed as it may be that in 98.4 per cent of the calls attended by WAST, none of these patients demonstrated any obvious risk, or that the EMS staff attending considered or undertook the HITS assessment, but did not record on the PCR that they had done so. A comprehensive action plan has been formulated to address these questions and to investigate the potential lack of compliance.

It is interesting to note that on the DA2 assessment form currently utilised in some services there are only options to highlight if you are either 'Miss/Ms/Mrs'. There is no category which could be selected to indicate if the victim is male. Although statistics consistently demonstrate that 1 in 4 females, compared to 1 in 7 males, will experience some form of domestic abuse in their lifetime,[16] it remains an interesting assumption, or oversight by policymakers, that only women will be seeking assistance. It raises the question, 'Do we have different expectations of the male victim?' It is important to consider whether male victims should also get the RE. Research has suggested that males do not receive RE screening in a healthcare setting (Sullivan and Websdale 2006).

When discussing referrals with EMS staff, there seemed to be an overwhelming consensus that staff remain uneasy about approaching potential victims due to the sensitivity of the situation. Over a period of four months 50 EMS staff were approached and invited to enter into a discussion relating to their experiences of attending domestic abuse 999 calls. Of the 50 EMS staff approached, 32 consented to having their remarks anonymously recorded. The numerous comments were then grouped into common themes, as contained in Figure 5.4.

Question	Themes	Responses N = 32
What are the main problems that you face when responding to, or managing a suspected domestic abuse call?	Lack of expertise or knowledge about DA	32
	Worries about 'getting it wrong'	31
	Awkward questions may upset the victim	29
	Asking questions may make the aggressor worse when we leave	23
	Feeling like you are interfering in someone's private business	9
	Making things worse for the victim	11
	Worries about personal safety	10
Is there any additional guidance that you would like to have, which might assist you when managing these calls?	No	3
	Better support pathways	21
	Feedback about referrals would help us to know if we are 'getting it right'	16
	Updates on Trust performance in relation to other emergency services or ambulance Trusts	7
How do you think we can best support victims when we attend suspected DA?	Call the police	27
	Offer patient call-back advice (DA1 or 2)	32
	Ask victim what they want us to do	11
	No idea how to resolve the issues	8
	Take victim to hospital so that they are in a safe environment	28
General comments which relate to recurrent themes (one example of a comment has been provided, but others were made which can be placed into the same category)	People argue and then make up again	12
	Victims can lie to get sympathy	5
	Our main concern should be any children	8
	If she was that unhappy, she'd leave	2
	Its hard if you are a double (male) crew and the patient is female	22
	The police don't seem to want to help us, everyone wants to pass the 'ball'	26
	Lots of the time there is alcohol as well so it's hard to know what is going on	32
	I am just supposed to deal with injuries	18

Figure 5.4 Common themes arising from conversations with 32 EMS personnel

Note: Staff made numerous comments during conversations which will have contributed to more than one theme.

Quotes from EMS staff September–November 2012:

1. On one job I went to, the husband had run away before we (police and ambulance) arrived. The wife was in tears and begging us not to report the situation cos' he (husband) was (in the) police. There were kids there in the house and I should have made the (Safeguard and Welfare of Children) referral, they weren't hurt, but she was, but I felt sorry for her. They weren't scroats (rough family) they were tidy people (respectable). She said she only phoned 999 to scare him and make him go away, and then she doesn't want us to do anything! It's impossible for us sometimes, how do you help people, I really don't know what we are supposed to do.
2. It's the kids that I feel sorry for, adults can sort themselves out, kids just get dragged along in it all, but if I'm wrong, I've made it even worse. Next time we see her she could be really injured.
3. Trouble is we are ambulance. If you get involved in a domestic, and if you tell her she has to report the call as DA, you might be doing the wrong thing, then the police come along, someone gets in trouble and the next time they need an ambulance, they don't call for help.
4. We should give advice and let the patient make their own mind up what to do. Like the vulnerable adults referral, if they don't want help, give them support, but let them handle it.
5. If we encourage the patient to report the abuse, she may end up in a situation which she can't control. Social services get involved and then she is under all kinds of pressure to do this or that.
6. I don't think we should be asking everyone if they are being abused (HITS). If you try to make every patient feel safe and they trust you, if they want help, they will ask for it. If I start asking those questions, they will think I am judging them. Then we can't be trusted.
7. More stuff on telly, like the advert years ago about the little cartoon kid that was being abused (NSPCC[17]) loads of people talked about that, it caused a real stir. Make one about men who beat up their wives. Embarrass the ********** (expletive) abusers, put it up in pubs and on toilet walls, make people know that…'That's you!'…it's not on, it's wrong and it's you.

There was a general consensus that the South Wales EMS staff who participated felt confused and concerned about managing domestic abuse situations. Most staff who responded stated that they felt that discreetly providing advice was the right thing to do, but it was hard to gain agreement on how that should be done; leave a leaflet, carefully provide victim with a calling card with referral phone number on it, leave it as a verbal support, we were unable to reach a consensus.

Analysis of findings from Figure 5.4

Interestingly, 87 per cent of EMS staff who were approached to discuss their experiences of domestic abuse said that they felt they could best protect the victim by taking them to hospital, but with hospital EDs already at capacity, and often unable to appropriately manage even the very sick and injured, this would not seem to be the most suitable referral route. In 2012 it was not uncommon for patients with less urgent conditions to remain on ambulance vehicles outside ED units for periods which ran into hours at a time. Although this might be preferable to leaving the victim at home in a possibly dangerous situation, it does disable an ambulance response and mean that another 999 emergency will not have an ambulance as quickly as they require it.

Of the EMS staff approached 84 per cent felt that domestic abuse was a matter for the police, but an additional 81 per cent felt that the police and other services didn't want to be involved, they felt that domestic abuse situations were like a ball being passed from one service to another as no one really knows how best to 'sort it out'. It is concerning to find that 66 per cent of EMS staff stated that they did not know how best to support victims of domestic abuse, and 91 per cent expressed a concern about asking questions due to fears relating to making the situation worse, with 72 per cent concerned about aggravating the aggressor.

Surely the most alarming and concerning finding was that 100 per cent of the staff who were approached felt that they did not possess the expertise to appropriately manage domestic abuse situations, with the same number making some reference to the anxiety relating to alcohol and drugs, which were so often involved in domestic abuse situations that the complexity and danger of the circumstances were increased. It was felt by those who responded that this significantly complicated the ability of the EMS staff to manage such scenes, with 97 per cent of staff experiencing fears about actually making things worse due to the volatile nature of such stimulants when mixed with heightened human emotions. Despite the high percentage of staff expressing concerns about making things worse, only 31 per cent of EMS staff actually mentioned concerns relating to their own safety.

On a positive note, 100 per cent of the EMS staff approached did comment upon using the DA1 or DA2 as a means of offering support to the victims, however 25 per cent also commented in the same conversation that they felt they did not know how best to support victims.

Development of alternative pathway within Wales, DA pilot

In 2013 frontline EMS ambulance staff in South Wales, UK, participated in an alternative pathway pilot aimed at enabling domestic abuse victims to access support and guidance. The pilot was run in a joint collaboration with the All Wales Domestic Abuse and Sexual Violence Association. In conjunction with this pilot, stickers were placed on the back of the doors in every public convenience within South Wales.

6
Interviews with Professionals

Introduction

The clarion call of frontline service officers who respond to domestic abuse is that they are frustrated. This is expressed in two key ways: first, using the victim as a focus for all that is wrong with responding to domestic abuse, a perception that 'if only the victim would behave properly and support the frontline agenda, then most of the problems of domestic abuse would disappear overnight'; and second, that responders feel ill-equipped to deal with the ongoing situation because it is too sensitive. There is a perception that domestic abuse isn't really a police matter, but it is not anyone else's responsibility either. This is, of course, a skewed, but nonetheless real, perception of the problems, which has serious repercussions. We heard from professionals that a multi-disciplinary approach to domestic abuse training, and knowing what happens when other professionals respond would help them understand the wider *care pathway:*

> What do the police have, do they get trained? We (ambulance and police) should all get together and do case studies, so we know what all the services do, get consistent approach. Help each other, you know what I mean.
>
> We all try to do a 'bit', but if no one knows what 'bit' you've done, or even what your 'bit' should be, it won't work. No one talks to anyone else (ambulance, police and other support services), not even the electronic sources (record departments).

There is no reason why police officers or paramedics should feel overwhelmed by domestic abuse in particular. They deal with equally, or even more, distressing and serious matters as a routine part of their role. There is a dominant discourse in circulation, part of a powerful discursive formation, which constructs the problem of domestic abuse as being a problem of victim behaviour. It is supported by historical authentication through experiential narratives, cultural gravitas, and pseudo-scientific evidence. It doesn't challenge a single conservatively held belief and can often be presented as insight rather than rhetoric. We have talked widely about status and this way of 'knowing about' domestic abuse proliferates by relying on the low status of the abuse and the victim. In this chapter we reproduce some of the comments made to us by frontline professionals, they have not been selected for their peculiar insight but for their ubiquity. Each comment is representative of the general feeling as expressed by many frontline paramedics and police officers. It should be noted that there are some differences in perception between paramedics and police officers and any commonality is within a job role and not necessarily across different jobs; so most police officers agreed with other officers, and vice versa. However, victim culpability and abuser invisibility was a definite commonality shared across the services.

We noted in Chapter 4 that domestic abuse, or 'domestics' as they are known across the services, seems to be the responsibility of no one in particular. No service wants to own the concept of domestic abuse in their profile. It would be more accurate to characterise cases of domestic abuse as being hot potatoes, which are passed on to another service or department as soon as possible.

> the police call us as back-up, they hope that we will just take the woman to hospital and then their problem is sorted. (Paramedic)

Repeat calls are not received with a sense of urgency, but with a roll of the eyes and a sense of futility. One police support worker said 'to be honest, if it's a "domestic" you can hear everyone groan'. We have organised the comments into those themes most commented on and with the most feeling.

Reluctance to attend a domestic abuse call

> I'll tell you what the problem is, it's those on the frontline, they don't want to deal with it (domestic abuse), I'll say to them, you've got an MO for an arrest there, but they won't do it. (Control Room Officer)

This comment came from an experienced call handler/dispatcher who was very frustrated about the lack of interest amongst frontline officers in even attending domestic abuse calls. It was said that officers on patrol would try to get out of attending, pretend they had other things to do and, if they did have to end up attending, they would avoid arresting anyone or designating the call as high risk. This kind of attitude was reflected in comments from frontline officers about whether they were willing to get 'tied up' with prisoners; that is, getting involved with arresting someone for domestic abuse and then being trapped in a custody centre for hours while paperwork, interviews and so on are sorted. Many frontline officers felt that the effort they put into processing domestic abuse prisoners would be wasted when the victim withdrew her statement the next day, which was seen as somewhat inevitable. So there is a problem with the problem. Police officers don't want to attend domestic abuse calls in the first place. It was not just the perceived futility that underpinned this reluctance, but also a feeling that it wasn't proper police work:

> It's not our job to sort out people's arguments.
>
> We're not social workers. We are supposed to be enforcing the law, we are police.
>
> Half our time is wasted on people using us to get back at their partners.
>
> Look its just all about the cut and thrust of life.

Police seemed to see 'domestics' as frustrating and ultimately a waste of time, and not police work anyway. If this is the case, it's much more than a training issue. Some officers did articulate the view that they felt they didn't need or want training:

> I don't need any training, there's nothing you can tell me about domestic abuse, I've been dealing with it for years.
>
> I've been dealing with domestic abuse for 24 years, you can't tell me anything about it that I don't already know.

It is a problem that professionals do not always recognise abuse, or differentiate between arguments and abuse. Those officers who said that they knew everything were putting 'domestics' into one category and homogenising the problem. Identifying risk and recognising coercive control is a matter of training and experience. The research tells us that deaths as a result of abuse are not going away. Deaths do result because of domestic arguments, but it is rare. In most cases of domestic homicide there has been a history of control (Websdale 2010, Adams 2007, Stark 2007). The professionals' reluctance to listen to what the identified risk factors are and to rely on their own, often cynical, assessment was widespread in the interviews.

There was also a feeling that officers did not have enough time to attend domestic calls and lack of time was described as the 'elephant in the room'. Officers felt that the quality of service they offered was dependent on time and that victims did not understand this:

> You've got control in your ear telling you about other jobs.
>
> You're rushed from job to job.
>
> They [the victim] just don't care how busy we are.

With reduced frontline resources there is a lot of pressure on professionals to get from job to job quickly. Not only do they sometimes have a lot of calls backing up, they also have time constraints – those parameters within which they must arrive at a call in order to meet their targets. The pressure is heavy and further cuts will only increase the pressure:

> I'm not saying it was a waste of my time because it wasn't, but I was on this call (domestic abuse) for nearly four hours talking to her, doing the risk assessment, gathering evidence, you know. But that means really nearly the whole of my shift was spent on that one call. They put you under pressure to get free and on to the next job. Then if she withdraws then it feels like it was all a waste of time, even if it wasn't.

Many officers considered that victims were untruthful, ungrateful, and sometimes hostile. Far from officers being seen as the heroes of the hour, they felt they were disrespected and powerless, which added to their frustration:

> Stupid women, they won't help you. Sometimes they jump on your back to stop you arresting him. (Police Constable)
>
> She's going to end up dead. We keep telling her to leave, but she doesn't. One day we'll go up there and she'll be dead, bless her. (Police Sergeant)
>
> What if they have kids, they lie to you then cos' they are afraid of losing the kids, having them taken away. So they hide what is

going on, even if we know it's not true, you can't call them a liar. (Paramedic)

There is recognition here of the seriousness of the situation and that murder may be the outcome. It seems bizarre that this is not considered proper policing. But it has also been found that domestic homicide is generally not seen as being as serious as other forms of homicide, especially homicides between strangers. Domestic homicides routinely attract lesser charges, and lesser sentences (Monckton Smith 2012, Lees 1997). This view is true across the criminal justice system, and is not just specific to police officers. In the above comments the foolishness or untruthfulness of female victims is referred to in different ways. What is absent are comments on the abuser who, in one comment, has been identified as a potential murderer. In another comment the police had at least informally assessed the situation as high risk for homicide. They do not discuss whether they conducted a formal risk assessment on this victim or not, one would assume this was done. But it was another frustration for officers conducting risk assessments that they had no follow up, they did not know what happened afterwards:

> Where do the bloody (DASH) forms go? No-one tells us. What happens to them? (Police Sergeant)
>
> Sometimes you're really concerned, but you never know what happens to them after you've gone. Sometimes it would be nice to know.

If officers are to care there should be some form of follow up for them, so that they can see their actions have an impact. They should know that the time they spent on the risk assessment actually influenced ongoing support for the victim, or interventions with the abuser. Sometimes it would be good for officers to know that a victim eventually took their advice. Officers may not realise that women don't always leave at the point of violence because they are far more practical and realistic about how and when to leave (Kirby et al. 2014). If officers felt that their actions had outcomes, the feeling of futility might not be so strong. Paramedics also felt that they would like to have some feedback from their domestic abuse calls, and that this would help them know if they were getting things right (see Chapter 5).

The overwhelming attitude expressed was that female victims were a big problem, but no one made a critical comment about male victims of abuse. Whenever the subject of male victims was raised, the conversation was always about how difficult it was for male victims to admit they had been assaulted. There was never even a hint that male victims would lie about abuse, or were foolish and reckless with their lives. In fact, it was never really considered that their lives were at risk:

> It's really hard for blokes. It's their Mrs isn't it. How can you admit that she hits you?
>
> Men get abused too. It's worse for them, 'cos they feel small. They feel like they should be able to deal with it.
>
> I've seen some women hitting men, really hard too. What's he supposed to do? He can't hit her back can he?

A male officer disclosed to us that he was a victim of abuse and was clearly distressed at the memory. His story revealed that some of the actions of his female abuser were shocking and saddening. He never called the police:

> One day she just picked up all my stuff and dumped it in the front garden, then she told me to get out and sat laughing with her friends

Impartiality

This leads us on to another potentially difficult concept, impartiality. Police officers said that in a 'domestic' they should remain impartial. This is a much bigger issue than it might appear. An emergency response is not necessarily the appropriate place for impartiality; that may be an interview or court room. In an emergency situation where the victim *needs* to be believed, impartiality can be extremely damaging. Women are three times more likely to be arrested for domestic abuse (Hester 2013b) to show that the police are taking their impartiality seriously and making sure they don't just arrest men. It could be that believability is more important than impartiality. Police also said to us that sometimes it is difficult to recognise who the offender is. This is about training. Officers should be able to recognise that the majority of control and abuse will be male on female. Where there is a history of abuse then impartiality is actually dangerous, what the victim needs is support, to be believed and to be made safe. A history of abuse should, at the very least, suggest that the victim is to be believed.

Our research shows that police officers are quite confident they know about domestic abuse, but we suggest that this might actually be clouding their perceived impartiality. The dominant discourse discriminates against females as victims in many ways, as discussed in Chapter 2. There is definite discrimination against female victims and little or no focus on the *ongoing* dangerous behaviour of the perpetrator. So, first, we would question whether impartiality is good in an emergency situation and, second, we would question whether impartiality is actually achieved. There are a high number of cautions and NFAs (no further action) for what are criminal actions, and this was revealed in the recent HMIC (2014) report on the responses of all forty-three police services to victims of domestic abuse. The report was published in March 2014 and found poor service for victims right across the country, with only eight of the forty-three police services providing good service. The report raised the issues of overuse of cautions, NFAs and not giving 'domestics' high status. The impartiality position may encourage the NFA or maybe a caution, if any action is taken at all. Also, impartiality implies that officers will respond to what they see at the time, this is problematic, for the victim may easily come across as the problem and the real abuse be completely missed.

In Chapter 2 we discussed anti-female bias and in interviews and focus groups officers, paramedics and others frequently want to tell us that men are abused as much as women and that it is domestic violence experts, or specialists, whose perceptions are being manipulated by women who just want to get back at their partner. This is part of the dominant discourse.

> Some women love the drama. The weekend is measured upon the amount of drama that can be created and then the amount of sympathy that the week then brings. No one puts up with being battered, if you want to get out there is always a way. It makes you wonder, what are we supposed to do? (Paramedic)

The argument of impartiality then takes on a new dimension. Impartiality evolves in conversations as a default position of 'not taking the woman's side'. In part this is a backlash against some feminist arguments, it is also in part a result of encouraging practitioners to see domestic abuse as gender neutral. This position enables professionals and others to recognise both atypical victims and any bias against other types of victim. So, for example, this argument says that professionals should be aware that same sex couples may have domestic abuse in their relationship and that, in some cases, men can also be victims of domestic abuse. But what seems to be happening is that this argument, meant to highlight an amount of victim diversity, is being misinterpreted or used to mean that the spread of victims will be equal. In terms of gender this just doesn't work. Most of our time in the interviews and focus groups was given over to trying to show that women are abused with far more regularity, and with far more sinister and dangerous outcomes, than most men. In terms of the statistics the problem is not gender neutral. It never has been. The problem is not just with police officers and paramedics, we have come across this argument from coroners, magistrates, judges, MPs and from non-professionals. The cultural leaning towards disbelieving women is seriously problematic when dealing with domestic abuse. We would argue that when a police officer attends a 'domestic' they do not exercise impartiality, but recognise, as professionals, that women are far more likely to be the victims of serious long term manipulation and abuse, even if they don't look like perfect victims at the time.

Instead, we have a situation where police officers do not use an evidence base for their attitude or decisions and behave as if they were arbiters in an equal dispute between consenting participants:

A You have to be impartial when you go to a domestic. You can't take sides.
Q Why not?
A Because you have to stand back and not get involved. You can't take sides.
Q Are you impartial in other forms of abuse and assault, or other crimes like robbery?
A That's not the same.

It seems that 'domestics' are a distinct category of police work which necessitates not taking the side of the victim, which is possibly not the usual stance taken in other cases of assault, like robbery or burglary. The victim in a 'domestic' is seen as culpable. It's almost as if the professionals are arbiters rather than law enforcers or safeguarders. The very term 'domestic' has a history to it, it is a discourse in itself, but police did not necessarily feel comfortable actually defining what a domestic is:

Q You keep referring to domestic abuse calls as 'domestics'. What is a 'domestic'? Can you tell me what it looks like?
A silence for some time
Q What are you expecting when you get sent to a 'domestic'?
A Well it's when there's trouble or violence, when it's families, well usually husband and wife. But it could be mother and son or

something, you get your domestics, they're not the same as like an assault, or a criminal damage.

Q Well those are crimes, are domestics not crimes then?

A They can be, it depends.

Invisible perpetrators

There was also a feeling that 'domestics' were all about awkward victims. Perpetrators were not talked about very much, and they certainly did not come in for the criticism that victims did. There was only one comment out of all the interviews and focus groups, where a police officer spoke negatively about perpetrators.

Q Can we talk about the perpetrators for a minute? What do you do with them?

A You might arrest him, but you split them up. Get him away from her, and see if you can get her to talk, see if she will fill out the DASH with you. But you need to get him out of the way. You need to sit with her and talk to her.

Q Yes, but let's talk about him for a minute.

A But it has to be victim focused, we're told all the time – it's got to be victim focused.

There was a reluctance to talk about perpetrators, the discourse was of victims. The perpetrator was a shadowy figure in the background, very much an extra in the production. The victim was the central player, and she was often both victim and problem. Criminal justice procedures were the subject of criticism. Police processes and expectations, lawyers, and even family members all came in for criticism. The offender was conspicuous by his absence. There were no strong feelings about him, and certainly no feeling that he was the problem, the serial abuser, the social evil. He was most in evidence when he and the victim were considered to be 'as bad as each other'. But as a criminal, as a dangerous, violent or abusive individual, he was quite inconspicuous. Police officers did talk about arresting him, where they had the power, but this was often said in the context of the victim's demeanour, and whether she was willing to support a prosecution. In most other crimes the police will focus on the offender, they will search out evidence and start an investigation (Monckton Smith et al. 2013), but in domestic abuse they take a different approach.

If she won't give a statement, what can we do, our hands are tied.

> We don't want to be criminalising men for domestics, it's not always as simple as you people make it out to be. (Criminal Justice Professional)

> I think it's dangerous to have a positive arrest policy. In the past hundreds of men have been locked up for this, that didn't do any good. Filling up the prisons with, well not criminals are they. (Criminal Justice Professional)

Paramedics must make life or death decisions both as a routine part of their job and often in high pressure situations. It is interesting that some feel that they don't want to make those decisions with regard to risk assessment in domestic abuse. It is suggestive again of the way professionals do not want responsibility for domestic abuse.

The routine argument is that specialist training is needed to 'deal' with domestic abuse. But this is a little misleading as 'dealing' with the ongoing abuse doesn't appear to be part of the first responder remit, their job is to assess the risk, identify offences, protect life and property, and then refer on to specialists as necessary. This is the same for any call for service, not just domestic abuse. The problem appears to be in recognising that there is a victim, and what the risk to that victim is. In this respect officers do need training.

> Q What do you do with the perpetrator?
> A Well we arrest him if we can.
> Q What if you can't, what do you do then?
> A To be honest, nothing really. What can you do? There is nothing, no programmes or anything.

Officers and paramedics were more confident dealing or talking with abusers when they could focus on a professional response like an arrest, or treatment of an injury. They had no confidence speaking with victims or abusers without these actions. It also appeared that where there was no serious injury or arrest that the 'domestic' call was treated as an argument which was a drain on their resources

> The trouble is bloody Facebook. The amount of domestics that are about things said on Facebook. Turn the bloody thing off, change your name, whatever. Just deal with it. The amount of time we waste on Facebook arguments is ridiculous.

Are officers really comparing coercive control and domestic abuse, to calls about arguments between friends or neighbours about Facebook?

Are officers hearing that Facebook is being used, and then giving the call such low status that they don't take anything seriously or even hear any of the ongoing history. It is concerning that officers may be putting all 'domestics' into one category or group and then fail to recognise serious abuse and risk or dangerous offenders. They are not differentiating between arguments and abuse.

Who owns domestic abuse?

Paramedics had frustrations with domestic abuse too. Some of their frustration was in feeling that domestic abuse was not their job.

> If there is violence, it's the police that should deal with it, not us.
>
> We try to be sympathetic, but we don't really have training how to 'manage' the 'feelings' of the patient.

In these two comments paramedics express that domestic abuse should be dealt with by the police or, perhaps, an even more specialist agency trained to deal with 'emotions'. Police officers do not necessarily see themselves in a caring function, they see their role predominantly as law enforcement. Paramedics are much closer to the caring role and may have fewer problems feeling or expressing sympathy with the victim as part of that role. However, some felt that it was more of a police responsibility to deal with domestic abuse. Police officers have often complained that they are not social workers, and that domestic abuse is a social rather than a criminal problem. Despite this police do recognise the potential risk to victims when they complain about them failing to leave an abuser. Paramedics openly articulate worries that they are not experts, and that is one reason they do not feel it is their responsibility:

> That's not our job, we aren't trained to do it, we are not the experts.... what if I report something and I am wrong, that's not my job, it's not my business.

In sharp contrast, police officers often felt they were expert, but expert in recognising how everyone else is manipulated by a false impression of the real problem. Domestic abuse is constructed as a problem caused by women. And, therefore, not a real criminal or health issue. In the research reported on in Chapter 5 paramedics commented that the police were not helpful to them and just wanted to pass the ball. But others felt it was not part of their job, and they should only be required to deal with injuries, not get involved in the context of those injuries, and leave the ball with the police.

She should just leave

Paramedics were just as likely to express the belief that women should just leave the relationship, first responders and people generally do not understand why victims don't always leave:

> If you are not happy, you just leave, surely that's what you do. I know it isn't quite that simple, you got to have somewhere to go of course, but you make plans, and you leave. (Paramedic)
>
> You try and tell them (to leave), but they don't listen. (Police)
>
> She had two good legs, she could have just left. (Police about deceased victim)
>
> If it was really that bad they'd just leave wouldn't they? It can't be that bad. (Police)

Not only was there a frustration with victims for not leaving, but a sense that the reasons for not leaving revealed the true nature of the problem. For example, that the problem could not be as bad as the victim made out, or that the victims were just foolish:

> She was just using him for his money. She kept complaining that he beat her but she still went shopping with him, let him buy things for the house. She was using him. If she was serious she would have left. (Police Investigator talking of murder victim)
>
> If she was really scared she'd have left the area. She could have left (location) and gone somewhere far away. She wasn't really serious, she wasn't that scared. (Police about deceased victim)

This comment doesn't really make sense. This victim had separated from her abuser but was living in the same town/city as him. The officer is saying that the victim was somehow trying to lead the police to believe that she was more frightened than she actually was. But the victim was right in her assessment because she was dead, killed by the abuser. So, in what respect was she untruthful? Her fear was realised, she was killed. So the threat was real, the victim had said she was scared, but the whole assessment of her relies on the idea that if she was really scared she'd have done more to protect herself, and that would have been by leaving the area so her abuser couldn't find her. This would have meant leaving her friends and family too. The officer is saying that she wasn't scared enough, and this takes some responsibility from their shoulders. Because, if she wasn't really scared then this murder wasn't actually predictable, and they are excused from blame. But it also implies that the police did all they could, her own actions got her killed. There is no blame on the police and no discussion of the abuser's blame. It was her responsibility, her fault.

Professionals as victims and abusers

During our interviews we came across a number of police officers who were victims of abuse. All but two of these officers were female. One of the officers said of her own experience of police responses, and her experience of working with colleagues on domestic abuse calls:

> I truly believe that they (police officers) don't care. They just don't care about domestic abuse or the victims. What they (police) forget is that victims are weak. It's really hard to leave, you're really beaten down.

Generally speaking, officers who were suffering abuse did not feel supported by their organisation, but did feel personally supported by colleagues. So there was more sympathy from colleague officers as individuals or friends than as professionals. The issue of impartiality came up again in this context:

> Well I suppose it's hard for them, they can't be seen to be taking my side. That might look bad for them. It's difficult.

We feel it important to comment on the idea that victims felt supported by their colleagues as individuals, but not by the organisation, and not by their colleagues as professionals. So, on a personal level officers would express sympathy and support for their colleague (as victim), but when dealing as professionals with the officer's actual problems they were not supportive. Was that to do with the feeling that they should be impartial, even where they had personal knowledge and a history of the situation? We also observed in talking with victims that they reverted to the language of 'domestics' when talking about domestic abuse calls they might attend themselves, or that others might attend. The institutional discourse of domestics is so powerful that it actually overshadows personal assessments, and personal experience.

Our conversations about the police potentially having abusers in their midst were not received with ease. This is understandable to an extent as it is not comfortable to think that colleagues you may have to rely on are potentially abusive at home.

> Q Obviously there will be some abusers who are police officers, do you take this into consideration when you think about training and specialist teams?
>
> A (shouting) How dare you, how dare you say such a thing. You'd better have some bloody good research to back up what you just said. That's an outrageous accusation. How dare you say that.

The thought that a police officer could also be an abuser was so repugnant to this officer that he became very aggressive. This same officer did recognise that some police officers would be victims. What is concerning in this exchange is not just the aggression in the response, though this is concerning in itself, but the intransigence. It is reported by victims that abusers frequently manipulate police officers into believing that the victim is the problem, it is also accepted by police officers that this happens. It is concerning that these officers may well take a complaint of abuse against another officer. The thought occurs that the victim would not be believed and this is also concerning. It has been shown in studies that police officers have a higher than average amount of abusers in their number (Lonsway 2006).

Domestic Abuse Case Study 7: Graham (Ivor) Jones

Ivor Jones was a police officer with 20 years of service who abused and controlled his wife Maria. He said that he discovered an affair and stabbed her 96 times in a jealous rage after she allegedly taunted him. Jones had repeatedly threatened to kill her, he had said, 'If I can't have you no one can', a known attitude of domestic killers. There were also stepchildren in the home. She was so terrified of him that she kept a knife under her pillow. It was this knife which killed her. Despite this terror of Jones, which the judge said was justified, the judge and media also believed that Maria had the courage to taunt the man who so terrified her. From what we know of women who suffer chronic fear as a result of abuse, this is a bizarre belief. However, the judge sentenced this man to only eight years. He will probably be released in half that time. This is an example of criminal justice solidarity with the killer blaming the victim.

Convincing women to support a prosecution

We spoke with a number of victim service teams who work with the police. These teams were in sexual assault referral services and domestic abuse support services. They were not staffed by police officers but by specialist victim support practitioners. These services had the appearance of 'women's aid' type services, but were not charities. Certainly, victims believed these services were there with their best interests at heart. We were surprised to learn that their predominant function was to make sure victims were encouraged, cajoled and urged to follow through with prosecutions. That was their purpose. We found that although the workers were sincere in their belief that they were a support service for victims, with a similar profile to an aid charity, they aggressively followed a separate organisational agenda:

> Sometimes it's really hard to convince her to go ahead with it, but we just keep at it. I will contact a victim once a week to convince her if I have to.
>
> They don't always want to go to court, but it's for the best, I really believe that.

They told us how hard it is sometimes to convince a woman to pursue a prosecution, but that they would persevere. They would call victims regularly, escort them to court, and make sure nothing happened to change their mind. But when asked what support they gave after court they admitted that their responsibility ended at the point of a court decision:

> Once we've got our court result, that's the end of our job really. We don't have anything to do with it after that.

When asked what happened if there was no conviction we were told that they always prepare the victim for a possible not guilty finding so they are not too distressed. We were told that they would be very positive about the upsides of a not guilty finding:

> We prepare them for the not guilty, just in case. I have my little speech already prepared, that I always use. I tell them that at least she showed him that she's not messing around, she really means it, she's let him know that she'll go through with it if he touches her again.

We found the whole model made us slightly uncomfortable, because the agenda did not include safety as clearly as prosecution. The institutional agenda was the *only* agenda in reality. We did not find the support workers to be uncaring, they genuinely believed that prosecution was the best support they could offer. This approach has some support and Stark (2013) argues that there are better outcomes where a prosecution is pursued, and that police should pursue prosecutions aggressively. This may be for many reasons, and may have much to do with a victim's determination to change things, or the deterrent effect on some men of punishment and formal repercussions when a conviction is achieved. Support staff did acknowledge that sometimes women could not be convinced to support a prosecution, and that perhaps it wasn't the right time for them:

> It's not always the right time for a woman to go to court, some of them you can tell it's not right, so you don't push it.

Even though the support workers were very motivated and believed in their mission, they were not able to provide any evidence, even anecdotal, that prosecution stopped the abuse or kept women safe:

> Q Do prosecutions stop the abuse do you think?
> A I think they do. I don't really know actually, but I think it sends the right message, it tells them that she will see it through, that she's serious.

Some stories told to us by support workers were inspirational. It was absolutely clear that a network of help is often available, with people who were prepared to go the extra mile for abused women. We have heard stories of some truly fantastic actions by the forced marriage unit for example, and domestic abuse charities being incredibly imaginative and helpful in facilitating escape from abusers. The police support staff were sincerely supportive and understanding of victims, and it has to be said we also came across police officers who were determined to do everything they could to help victims. It was often frustration with the criminal justice system further along which was evident, as it could undo so much of the support and work already done to try and help victims escape abuse.

It was a problem for some officers and support workers that the wider criminal justice system was unpredictable, and that CPS lawyers and judges, magistrates and juries were not always supportive or helpful, and frequently had little knowledge of domestic abuse:

> I got her to agree to go to court, and then the bloody CPS lawyer said, no its all summary offences. The man had strangled her, he had held a knife to his kid's throat, he was out after three weeks because it was just summary offences.
>
> The CPS said it was just trivial. Do you know what he did, he broke into her house whilst she was out and he left his item of property on the coffee table. Then he left. She was terrified. He knew that, he did it on purpose, he planned that. CPS said it was not serious enough for charge, but he's stalking her. They don't think it's serious.
>
> We interviewed this woman because her child had disclosed to the school about awful abuse. When we started interviewing her (the mother) she told us all about this plan she had to kill him. Just came right out with it. Thankfully she wasn't arrested or anything.

This raises an important point. It is futile to train frontline officers to respond properly to domestic abuse if the professionals in the rest of the system do not also have that training. There is an urgent need for all professionals to recognise abuse and be united in trying to end it. Domestic Homicide Reviews routinely identify terrible practices and attitudes in many more organisations than the police. We do suggest interagency training to align priorities and share practice to give confidence in the system. We discuss this further in Chapter 9.

In conclusion, when talking to police officers we found that they largely share the same frustrations, the differences were noticeable in the way individual officers processed ideas about where that frustration came from. Some officers were frustrated with the system, with the abuser and with constant battles that hampered attempts to help victims escape; others were frustrated that the victim wouldn't help them with their institutional agenda, failed to see their own shortcomings, and failed to comprehend that someone could be in genuine fear.

We feel that having spoken with so many officers that there is a genuine desire to help victims escape abuse. It is not that officers do not care, but that they don't always recognise those who need the most care. We feel that if there was more knowledge, there would be more understanding. This knowledge will come through training and applying evidence based practice. Sometimes officers are more motivated by evidence based recommendations than by being told to sympathise when they're not convinced the victim deserves sympathy. Evidence based policing is seen as the way forward and this should perhaps form a part of their training. We have observed that much police training involves being told to do something without being told why. Police officers are good at training other police officers to be police officers, but specialists need to deliver evidence based research, especially to let police officers know why they are being asked to complete risk assessments in the way they are.

Domestic Abuse Case Study 8: Charlie Sheen

Hollywood actor Charlie Sheen is reported to have a long history of violence against women. Former wives and girlfriends have made allegations, some of which he has admitted to. Much of the time he was reported as calling his accusers liars or fantasists. Certainly, his domestic abuse has not been as high profile as his career, the same has happened with OJ Simpson and others. Many high profile individuals have been accused of domestic abuse, and this would be good opportunity for society to express its denunciation of this practice. It rarely happens. Other high profile names who have been accused of domestic abuse include: Paul (Gazza) Gascoigne, singer Chris Brown, Charles Saatchi, Ike Turner, Mel Gibson, Alec Baldwin, Bobby Brown, James Brown, Josh Brolin, Sean Penn, Nicholas Cage, Mickey Rourke and Phil Spectre.

7
Interviews with Victims

Her strategy

In this chapter we are going to discuss the victim of abuse from her own perspective. We asked victims about their experiences of abuse. We wanted to know what abuse looked like from the inside and how it was managed. We wanted to hear as much as possible about how they managed their own safety. Police and others have said that victims are a problem and do not always respond the way that you might expect them to. So this was a priority for us, to attempt to gain some insight by looking at the decisions victims made on a day to day basis. We also spoke with relatives and friends of deceased women about what they witnessed, or may have been told, about safety planning. We have to respect the anonymity of our interviewees. Just speaking with us has put some women in danger so we have not revealed anything about them. We have changed some of their words as further protection. For example, the gender of children or the number of children, we have also removed mentions of specific injuries or events which might identify a woman. This means that the horror of some abuse is not visible, as we just can't be that specific.

For many years criminal justice professionals and others have been talking about their frustration with victims of domestic abuse. In fact, two key complaints about victims have dominated perceptions of abuse victims for at least thirty years. As a police officer in the 1980s I was introduced to the world of 'domestics' with the problems framed around two key complaints: 'Why doesn't she just leave?' and 'What's the point of doing anything, she'll just withdraw her complaint in the morning?' Those two complaints still dominate popular understanding of the challenges of responding to domestic abuse and are a product of the dominant discourse of IPA. I remember my horror at attending a domestic abuse call when I was a young police officer. A young woman had been hit in the head with a lump hammer by her abusive boyfriend. He had fled the scene. She would not even allow paramedics to take her to the hospital, let alone make a statement to the police so that they could start a prosecution. She was quiet and subdued, beaten and injured, but would not be convinced to support the police or paramedic agenda. We left her alone, claiming there was nothing we could do. I was told how this happened all the time, that victims were just awkward and that I would have to get used to it. There was no more conversation about that young woman and I don't know what happened to her. It was a sobering experience for me, a 19-year-old woman myself.

The memory still haunts me and I think that we should stop relying on the 'victims are awkward' explanation to rationalise what is really happening. This woman probably would not have refused paramedic intervention had she been involved in a car accident. She would not have refused to make a statement to police if she had suffered a burglary or robbery. She didn't just have an inexplicable lack of consideration for her own health and happiness, and sense of justice. She was not so mentally ill that her own health meant nothing. She fed herself, kept herself warm, dressed, washed and drank. After we left she probably tried to patch up her injuries with bandages and antiseptic. She did care about her health and wellbeing. So what stopped her from allowing the police and paramedics to help her? It's not because she was awkward. The usual explanation is that she is too frightened to let someone else care for her. But even this needs much better understanding, she was more than merely frightened. She was weighing up the repercussions of accepting help and, on balance, she thought it safer to look after her injuries herself, and get the police to leave. That is a remarkable decision; pragmatic and eminently logical, but fraught with danger. Her injuries could be life threatening, but on balance keeping him happy was more important. She was bartering with her life, not a position that either the professionals or the abuser were in. She decided that her injuries were less dangerous than he was. To describe this young woman as being awkward, or stupid, or frustrating, or reckless, does not recognise the sense of what she was doing as she saw it.

Ask not why she doesn't leave, but how can we make it safe for her to leave. Make it safe for her to receive medical help. One woman said to us:

> He's broken my fingers, and my ribs. He's given me black eyes and pushed me down the stairs. I try not to go to the doctor, and I never call the police.

From the outside the point of view is very different. For example, the paramedic who is called by police to assess a victim after the neighbour complains about a disruption might have a very different viewpoint:

> She is standing there with her hair all over the place, shaking like a leaf and telling us that everything is fine, that the neighbour is just interfering. She didn't want an ambulance, so now we have to fill in loads of paperwork 'cos we can't just leave, we are not allowed to do that. We complete the refusal to travel paperwork, but you know its all rubbish, she is lying to protect 'what'? I don't know. Why doesn't she just come with us, get out of there?

In a recent academic paper I was reviewing, female victims of domestic homicide were described as reckless for being in the same room as their killer; I heard a senior police officer say of a murdered woman that she had used the killer for his money because he bought things for her household; I heard prosecuting counsel describe a deceased woman as 'foolish' for allowing her killer into her home; I heard that a police officer told the relative of a deceased abuse victim that 'she had two legs she could have walked away'. Some things have not changed in the last thirty years. It does not occur to any of these people that domestic abuse victims are constrained in the amount of space they have for action, or that their choices are unusually limited. It would be more productive if those who uttered the two complaints we have described, realised that allowing an abuser into her home was a safety strategy for a victim of abuse, a strategy which may have kept her alive for years. Denying him access with no support would be far more dangerous.

> If I didn't let him in, he'd probably just get in anyway. Then I'd be up to my eyes in it. It keeps him calm if I just go along with it, you know.
>
> We're not even together any more. But I'm not going to push my luck. I let him come in and have a cup of tea. Sometimes he sees the grandchildren. I daren't have a partner, a boyfriend. He'd go mad. No, at the moment it's okay, I just keep him sweet.

In most cases, leaving the abuser will not stop the abuse. On its own, as a tactic, it is neither effective nor successful. In fact, it is well known that it is the single most dangerous thing an abused woman can do (Stark 2007, Richards 2006, Websdale 1999, Polk 1994). So why would a rational and informed professional expect her to? We considered how women managed a dangerous man on a day to day basis. We wanted women to talk about how they did it. Abused women know the abuser best. They know what he is capable of, they know how it looks when he's getting dangerous. Outsiders do not always know. So, if the victim knows him the best, we must listen to her to inform a safety plan we formulate with and for her. It became very clear, very quickly, that all the women and families we spoke with talked about the same basic safety strategy. They realised, even if it wasn't fully clear as a thought, that the only person who could really ensure their safety was the abuser himself. Police attitudes were unsupportive in many cases, and the tools they had to deal with the abuser were not powerful enough to remove her fear:

> What can the police do? If I take their side, he'll just come back in the morning madder than before.
>
> She always lied to the police, she would never admit he was abusive, she would say everything's fine, and tell them to go away and leave her alone.
>
> She left him, and she begged the police for help. They just didn't take her seriously.

According to our research the most common safety strategy employed by domestic abuse victims is to demonstrate love, loyalty and devotion to appease the abuser. To achieve this they must give the impression, true or not, that they love him, respect him, and want him squarely in their lives and their homes. Abusers always seem to require that the object of their abuse declare and demonstrate love and devotion. As discussed in earlier chapters, abusers are often dysfunctional and unable to handle rejection. They are frequently on a psychotic or psychopathic spectrum and in need of support or control themselves (Brown et al. 2013).

> He has to think I love him more than anyone else, you know, even more than the children or my mum.
>
> I used to agree with him when he said nasty things about my close friends or family, because if I disagreed, he would go into a rage and accuse them of turning me against him. If I went out with friends he would always turn up, just appear watching me, to protect me he'd say, then there would be an argument because he'd pretend to have seen something that just didn't happen. To test me, to make me admit something, so I stopped going out with my friends, it just wasn't worth it.

Nearly all victims said that behaviours deemed by him as not giving sufficient love and devotion would trigger escalated abuse, or abuse would start with the explicit suggestion that she should be more devoted. For example, 'If you loved me you wouldn't have said that or done that.' Or, she would have to say things like, 'I love only you, I don't ever look at other men.'. She would have to happily seek and follow his advice, and remember everything that pleases him. She knows this, she lives with this requirement. So she has a strategy that she will appease him, and keep herself safe by demonstrating devotion. He gets more dangerous the more he feels her attention and devotion is not his, some abuse is to make her declare and reaffirm that love.

> I make him think I love him. if I don't I've had it.
>
> The police can't help me, no one can. He would say I'm mad or something and have the kids taken away from me. I have to behave, I have to pretend I am the loving wife. I don't love him.
>
> I used to say 'aww babe, I love you, I can't live without you babe' and he'd just been hitting me, and there I was telling him I loved him. But it was the only way to, like, get him to stop.
>
> He would kick off and I would have to chase after him and tell him how much I loved him, I would have to keep saying it and saying it 'til he stopped. He would sulk for hours, but if I could convince him I loved him it might be alright.
>
> At a party he caught me talking to a friend, a male friend. He kicked off and shoved me down the stairs. I was really fed up, I felt stupid, everyone was looking at us. But I still had to go and tell him I was sorry and that I loved him.
>
> It was always the same, a pattern. He would suddenly go all sulky or maybe angry and then the only thing would be to treat him like a child and tell him how much I loved him. Sometimes it was easier than others, but it was the only way to stop the crap.
>
> I had to say he was the only man for me, I had to keep saying it or he would get angry, he hated the cat, I used to put her out, and then I'd tell him I loved him.
>
> Standing in a pub once, just talking to him and having a nice time, out of the blue he accuses me of looking over his shoulder at another bloke! The whole evening was ruined, he was so angry and would not see how ridiculous it was. Only telling him, reassuring him that no one else is good enough, that he is the only one, does any good when he gets like that.

He's always there

This strategy, to make him believe she loves him, is supported in research which suggests that men who abuse cannot handle rejection (Brown et al. 2010, Websdale 2010). In this respect the woman's strategy exactly matches his problem. But it is quite a fragile strategy and he will be looking for proof all the time that she is devoted to him. Sometimes she is stalked and surveilled, he will check her phone, her computer, he may listen to all her conversations. If she slips, if he thinks she is lying, she may put herself in danger. Some women reported to us that they just tell everyone they love him. It's safer:

> I tell everyone I love him. He's not stupid. How stupid would I be if I told the police I hated him? I tell the police I love him, it's the only way to get them to leave me alone. That time when I said to police, go on then I'll make a statement, and then I was in the house on my own. I don't know where he was. But it was better to have him here where I could see him, better than wondering. I just said to the police, I love him, and I've forgiven him.

One victim was talking about an incident where she accidentally disclosed to the head teacher of her child's school that her child may have witnessed abuse of her. The head teacher told her that he was going to inform social services as that was now considered abuse of the child. The woman immediately panicked and withdrew her statement:

> I just had this premonition that they would write it down somewhere that I had accused him of something, of domestic violence. I denied it, in fact I got really angry with the head teacher and told him he didn't know what he was doing. I said that he (abuser) had never touched me ever. I had to try and get him to believe me, to think I had been lying, otherwise he would just write it down. I had to stop him, I was panicking. He still called social services and I had a home visit. I had to trust that the kids wouldn't tell him about it. I was panicking, I still panic about it.

Without confidentiality disclosure of abuse may be dangerous, and women will have little incentive to tell anyone (Lindhorst et al. 2008) As in this case, the woman was not only frightened that her abuser might find out that she had spoken badly of him in public, but she was also terrified that her children would be taken by social services. This is a common fear for women, and a very real one (Lindhorst et al. 2008). This woman will never disclose domestic abuse again after the reckless behaviour of this head teacher. In many circumstances it becomes clear why women lie and protect their abuser, they may well prefer to keep it secret. Professionals rolled their eyes as they told us stories of abused women declaring their love for the abuser. But they fail to consider anything other than weakness as the explanation. Stark (2013) notes that everything becomes a test of her devotion for him. He watches her, her strategy must be bomb proof. Why would she say anything else?

The biggest trigger for domestic homicide is when she wants to separate (Stark 2007, Richards 2006). A separation is the ultimate declaration that she is *not* devoted to him. For her safety strategy to work she has to openly ignore and reject all the help she is offered because her main and most effective strategy would be ruined if she did not. She knows if she appears to slip, or if he thinks she doesn't devote herself to him, or she doesn't love him enough, he will become more dangerous.

> He's stopped working, he just stays at home all the time. I'd leave if I could and he knows it. But I won't leave without my kids, so he always takes one of the kids with him wherever he goes so he knows I'll be there when he gets back.

So if we consider this we can start to understand the answers to our two questions: 'Why doesn't she just leave?' and 'Why doesn't she support a prosecution?'

If she did either of these two things she would be declaring that she was not devoted, that she didn't love him, and that's when he can turn really dangerous, or even into a killer. If she does feel, in the heat of the moment and whilst the police are there, that she can support a prosecution, this may not last. Once the police leave and she realises that she is alone, she may *reinstate her safety plan* and withdraw her complaint. This demonstrates to him that she loves him and she may feel much safer.

Domestic Abuse Case Study 9: Caroline

Caroline managed to leave her brutal husband by entering a refuge with her three children and divorcing him. She was terrified of him, but the judge granted him access to his children with no restrictions. Caroline felt she had to allow him into her home to see the children. He appeared to have 'moved on' because he had another live-in girlfriend. He began to spend more and more time at Caroline's house, started checking on her and exerting more and more control. The other woman is now gone and he is now living in Caroline's home. No one sees her any more, her family are banned from entry to the home. Caroline said at a health surgery where a snatched meeting happened that she can't leave him a second time, he has said he will kill her and keep the children. She is terrified for her children and herself. She says she won't trust the system a second time. Caroline's situation in ongoing.

Everything in life becomes a test of her devotion to him (Stark 2013). Even her being ill will be a test of her devotion, he may get threatened and jealous that he is not receiving her full attention. An abuser makes it so nothing is safe from him, he has access to everything about her, and everything she has is vulnerable. Her position is supported as valid by years of research and experience. The position that she should up and leave on her 'two perfectly good legs', is proven to be extremely dangerous. And once she has declared that she's not devoted, she's going to need a robust and ongoing safety plan in place. One of the biggest triggers for insecurity in an abuser, and a feeling that he needs to exert *more* control, is the interference of outsiders. There is no better example than attendance by the police. First, the police remove some of his power to control what is happening; and second, she will be required to make his worst fears come true and side with the officer. It's a game of sides for him. If we light the touchpaper to an emotionally unstable man, make him face his worst fear and then leave him and her alone to deal with it, we would be reckless wouldn't we? At the same time as triggering his most dangerous state we tell her she must abandon her safety plan, a plan she feels is the only thing that has a chance to keep her safe. She feels that he can keep her safer than the police. Pain states that 'fear is not just a by-product of domestic abuse, it's a key element that keeps it going' (2013: 14). As a police officer or other professional encouraging her to leave, consider this really important question: Can her fear of him match her trust in you?

> You feel like a fraud, you want them to be honest, to trust you, to confide in you, but what can you do then, what do you do with all of that information that you've just asked for? Give her a card with a few numbers on it and then you leave. No one really studies your paper work when you submit it, or what it says. You've just let her down too. (Paramedic)

You must convince her you can keep her safe, not just for the next 24 hours, or 24 days, but on into the future until the threat has disappeared. The first three months after leaving are statistically the most dangerous (Campbell et al. 2007), but some victims are killed after two years or more. The abuse will continue all that time, even if the two are estranged and he has a new partner. Stalking and child contact are often used to continue abuse. Many men have legitimate reasons to see their children, but questions should be asked about their motives where there has been a history of control and abuse. She will be under enormous pressure to manage her own safety. Police should also remember that in many cases he is more concerned with losing control of her than he is of being arrested or its consequences.

It is also important to ask the question 'What is safety?' Safety is more than being free from the immediate threat which you think you are dealing with, she must be made free of all threats:

> A&E is a place of safety, but what happens when they get sent home again. It might not help to call police or insist they go to hospital. It's not our choice. We could make things worse. (Paramedic)

Abusive men wield power in many different ways and they will use all the methods they can to regain control.

> When he used to say sorry, he would say that he only did these things because he loved me so much he could not control himself. The thought of losing me made him lose control.

Most women in the most danger know he is capable of killing her and they will often say it. Her biggest fear will not necessarily be the threat of violence. We must also consider that once she has abandoned her safety plan it may never work again, so she has to put her very life in the hands of a busy police officer with few tools to ensure ongoing safety and no power at all to promise that a judge won't give him access to the children, or free him immediately from custody. The question should be 'Why would she leave?' or 'Why would she support a prosecution?' Take a step back for one minute and think what the benefit is to the victim of supporting a prosecution. Will it stop the abuse? The answer is very probably not. Will it make her safer? The answer is probably not. Will it make him go away? The answer is very probably no.

Stark (2013) argues that there are better outcomes where a prosecution takes place, so it is important that victims are able to pursue prosecutions safely. For her to support a prosecution, her fear of the abuser must, at the very least, match her trust in the officer. We should, at the very least, give her the respect of accepting, in terms of her safety, that her strategy may be more effective than our strategy of prosecution. She knows, she's living with it. As victim's advocate Frank Mullane puts it: 'She's been dancing round a psychopath for years.' We aren't the focus for his campaign of terror, she is. Let's listen to her and how she needs to deal with his abuse because she's trying to manage him and us. If we want a prosecution, the biggest bar to that is him not her, we must start dealing with him.

He needs her. He is a man who struggles with challenges, cannot take rejection, and is threatened when he feels he does not have complete control (Brown et al. 2010, Websdale 2010, Stark 2007). As we have discussed, not all men who commit domestic homicide are the same, but there is one consistency across nearly all of them, they need to be in control. The most dangerous men will make sure they have control over the woman so that she doesn't leave. If she leaves, he does not walk away and accept it, he will exert control from a distance. This is why stalking is such a high risk characteristic. It isn't about romance or love, it's a desperate attempt to exert control. The stalking behaviour may be to frighten her, to let her know he is still in charge; it may be to surveille her so that he has knowledge of everything she does, and everywhere she goes; it may be to let her know that it's only over when he says it is; it may be to let her know he's going to get revenge; it will most likely be all of these things. It's a very frightening and debilitating strategy. Abusive men are obsessive, stalking is obsessive and should always be treated as a dangerous behaviour. Constant texting or calling is obsessive, leaving abusive messages is dangerous, following her to work is particularly dangerous.

> When the police checked with the telephone company there were over 100 calls to the address over a two-day period. Most of the calls only lasted seconds as he was shouting down the line at me and I was hanging up. He would also leave insulting messages on the answer machine, accusing me of betraying him if I didn't answer the phone or if I was out when he called.

There does not need to be violence, for there to be a threat to life. Some men will stalk their partners whilst the relationship is intact. They will follow, they will go through her Internet history, her phone and so on. This is dangerous behaviour:

> I came home one day and he was sitting in my front room. He had copied the key and had been going through my bins to see what I had been eating. He wanted to know why there were two dishes on the draining

> board, who had I been 'entertaining'? he had looked through my diary, even my laundry tub to check if I had worn anything pretty... he asked who was I trying to impress by wearing my new jeans?

The control is a process, women don't see the control and abuse on the first date. He doesn't let them see his insecurity straight away. It's a course of conduct practised over time to gain her trust first. It would be usual to start by being quite charming, for him to declare his love, and look for this to be reciprocated. Slowly the control would be instilled through seemingly innocuous behaviours, or through stated vulnerability. For example, on the night he knows she goes out with her friends or her family, he may turn up with chocolates and a video and look so disappointed that he 'remembers' she is going out. She may well cancel her night out with friends. He has got her to follow his will. This can slowly isolate her from friends and family. This often moves on to 'your friends hate me' or 'your family have never liked me', then going to see them is disloyal and difficult for her. She must choose between them. The closer the family, the more likely this is to happen because the potential for influence from the family is higher. Then she may never mention going to see friends or family because it's just too difficult. Then she is isolated from help:

> It started that he would say me mum didn't like him, then he'd get mad if I went to see her anyway 'cos that was me not being loyal to him. Now I just don't see her 'cos its not worth the fight, now he won't let her near the house 'cos she got mad with him about it. I just stay away now.
>
> She changed completely. We were such a close family, but she just stopped calling and coming to see us. We knew what he was doing to her, we even went to the police but they said there was nothing they could do. She would tell them she was fine. She would lie.
>
> It's not worth winding him up. It's easier to keep your head down and try to get on with everything. I just do as I'm told now. It's easier.

This may move on to him telling her she can't go because they hate him, to threatening to harm them if she does go. Sometimes not seeing family is to protect them. One of the interviewees had only one friend who was allowed access to her house

> My friend has to pretend she thinks he's great. She never speaks against him, or even gives him a funny look because if she did he would ban her from the house, he wouldn't let me be friends with her.

The Friend said:

> I hate him, I absolutely hate him, but I behave or he would throw me out and I'd never get back in.

This comment is from a man who has a daughter trapped with a severely abusive man:

> Now I understand why she won't talk to me. But it doesn't make it any easier. There's nothing I can do for her, I can't get in. I can't save her. He's banned us from visiting our own daughter.

Where isolation from family and friends has occurred there is very often control. If family are worried they should be taken seriously. This kind of information should support prosecutions and inquests, and would be very helpful in a risk assessment.

Trust in the police was articulated mainly from two angles. First, that victims didn't think the police would believe them, or that they felt police were not sympathetic:

> One night he was hitting me around and he just wouldn't stop, he was pulling my hair and hitting me. Someone called the police and it was just when they turned up that I hit him. I never hit him back. It was the first time but I just had enough, I just had enough. The police officer saw me hit him and I got arrested. He was really fuckin' me about. They believed him. He said I was a load of trouble. I got done for assault. Then I lost my kids. He's got custody because he hasn't got a record, he's a bastard and now I can't get a job working with children. That was my dream. It's not fair and no one cares a shit.

The second angle was that they didn't trust the police to be able to control him. They had no faith that the criminal justice system would actually do anything to help. Many victims had awful stories about abusers being released early, or with no charges. Sometimes they weren't even told in time before the abuser turned up at their home. There is quite a long way to go before victims will feel confident in the criminal justice response. It's not as simple as just the first response and getting him to stop at that point in time. Victims aren't stupid, they know an emergency response is a quick fix for immediate safety, but it has no ongoing value, to choose the long haul of a prosecution has little value for the victim.

> I think that we get called 'cos we can be sent away. If you call the police, you are stuck with them. We arrive and the woman says that she now feels better. He's ***** himself and is now behaving. I suppose she's bought herself some more time. I went to a call once where she denied even calling 999, but the call is logged, we know it was her. (Paramedic)

Some victims call because of violence, it's almost impossible to call on the basis of coercion and control. Other victims will call to try and manage stalking behaviour. As discussed, stalking is a very high risk behaviour, but police still don't take it very seriously:

> He's never hit me, but I always thought he might. He would follow me, and shout at me. It wasn't worth the hassle so I would just shut up and do as I was told. It would keep him happy, and if he was happy I felt safer. But when I left him he started stalking me. Now I have a panic alarm from the (women's aid) people, but no one believes me that one day he's gonna slit my throat.

Victims described to us a life of fear. They were constantly on trial, and the potential for the abuser to become nasty or emotional was different in different relationships, but the fear was always there:

> We used to sit and wait for him to walk through the door wondering what kind of a mood he was in. I could tell as soon as I saw his face what the night was going to be like. If he had that look, I would try to be really nice and sort of happy. If I stepped out of line I knew what would happen.
>
> He was horrible. He would come in and we would know what it was going to be like. Just one look at him. He wouldn't say anything. He would sit there in silence. The atmosphere was awful. Then he would start, not always, but if he did I used to just run up to my bedroom.
>
> He trapped us at the top of the stairs once. He had a gun, he wasn't pointing it at us, but he was angry and we were terrified. We just sat there absolutely still, wishing he would go out. There was no one we could tell. He would have come after me if I had done that.
>
> What do I do when I see that look? I have to tell myself to stay calm and just calm him down. I think I know what to do, but then he changes it. I think I know what to say, but sometimes when it's really bad I try not to look at him. He says I'm not grateful.

There is always the very sensitive question of the safety of children, who have even less power to make decisions about their own safety. Abused women are routinely severely criticised for putting their children in danger. Criticism of the abuser for *being* that danger is much less in evidence. We talked to women about their feelings about their children. They talked about this from two perspectives: how the children were used to perpetuate the fear; and how they felt about the safety of their children:

> If the kids are with me they're safer than if they're in care. I want them with me for the future, for all their lives. If he kills me they will go to him, I couldn't do that to them.
>
> If I leave we're all in danger, what choice have I got?
>
> If I leave him, I know what he'll do, he'll try and get custody of them. He doesn't really want to look after them, he wants to spite me. He could say I was mad or unfit or anything. They'll believe him, they always do. Can you imagine that? Them living with him, without me, I can't even think about that, I'd rather die.
>
> He said if I go he'll come and get the children. Just take them one day out of school. How do I know I can stop him? Some bloody judge somewhere will give him rights, then what can I do to keep them safe?
>
> If he's close I know where he is. I know it seems mad, but I don't want them to go into care. I will get away one day, and we'll be okay.
>
> If he kills me, he gets the kids. I take the beatings, if I left it wouldn't be beatings, it'd be the chop.

From these statements we felt that women had thought about the safety of their children, they just didn't think anyone would help them achieve safety. They were concerned that leaving could have three outcomes: getting killed; having the children put into care; or having him hurt or kidnap the children. From the outside this strategy doesn't look like the best one, but consider the alternatives. Social services do threaten to take children away from abused women. Their remit is the safety of the children, not the children and the mother. It would perhaps be better to recognise that what she is doing is a strategy, not that she is a one-dimensionally, self-interested, terrible mother. Sometimes it may be better to question her strategy, rather than her moral fibre. Work with her to find a better strategy. Being accused of being a poor mother is low status indeed for a woman. It is hardly ever recognised that she is trying to keep her children safe, even if it appears to be failing. We have heard many stories, and looked at many cases, where custody is given to the abuser. Even after a homicide custody is being given to the killer, or the killer's family. Again, her fear is justified and rational.

Most of the victims we spoke with wanted the abuse to stop and the relationship to end, they wanted the freedom to make choices for themselves again. Some did say that they would never admit to not loving him to anyone, because if he ever found out they would be in trouble. Some said they felt conflicted and didn't know how they felt most of the time. No victim who had managed to leave the relationship said they had any love for the abuser. They said that their thoughts were much clearer when they had the freedom to think about their lives without reference to their potential death. Another interesting point was that they were more willing to tolerate violence than control. Many victims said they forgave the violence, but the control was unbearable and unforgivable:

> One day I hope he will realise that he doesn't really love me and he'll just leave. He might even find someone else, and just let me go. I dream about that. The only way I'll be safe is if he leaves me, I can't leave him, he'll kill me.

8 The Lesser Status of Families

Despite significant improvements in the last few years to the way victims' families are treated after homicide, and the sensitive and caring attitude of many professionals who treat them with the respect and inclusiveness they deserve, their needs are still not intrinsically a part of many criminal justice and other state processes. The outcome for many victims and families is a status gap between them and those employed to carry out these processes.

> violent death is considered a public issue where the need for justice takes precedence over the needs of homicide families. (Armour 2002)

We have seen a revised victim's code, the appointment of a chief coroner, statutory domestic homicide reviews, the Crown Prosecution Service engaging with victim's families, and the appointment of a victim's commissioner. I have been party to discussions focusing on bringing in a victim's law. The law may enforce better treatment, but a sustained change in the status of these families will come from there being a sizeable shift in both the understanding amongst agency workers of how families should be treated, and then their willingness to act on that understanding.

My daily job often includes contacting agency workers, for example the chair of a domestic homicide review, to request an update to help a bereaved family hungry for information. Even a message that there is no news is valuable, and many chairs recognise this, but such information often has to be sought. It seems to me that these professionals would not be so slow to update the body that commissioned them, as that could mean they were not recommissioned, but there is no penalty for treating families with less reverence.

We also know from experience that most professionals care very deeply. As one family member told me:

> I am sure the police worked long hours on the case, went the extra mile and missed time with their families as a result. I imagine they were emotionally affected by the case.

But the same family member cautioned:

> But when you return to the house where your loved one died and find what you consider an article of key importance (a grab bag, ready for an escape) has not been removed as evidence – despite it being exactly where you said it would be, and being questioned about this, you begin to lose confidence.

That many professionals care deeply is most often demonstrated in face to face meetings. Having engaged over many years with a significant number of families who have suffered homicide, I suggest that demonstrating this care can have an important effect. Some people bereaved through homicide are comforted when they look into the eyes of an agency worker who really cares; perhaps some healing, however minor, takes place. This positive effect may also apply to officials as individuals, as well as to the relationship between victim and the state, especially where it is thought that the state has failed. In my experience, if officials are perceived by the family as being indifferent or insincere, even if, in reality, they are not, a negative effect is sometimes experienced by all concerned. This is a complex area that would benefit from skilled research.

It is important for those in the criminal justice system who meet families after homicide to be truthful, open and sincere, including when describing next steps. Trust is quickly broken if it is perceived that an official is being disingenuous and if, following a helpful meeting, promised actions are not taken and the agencies do not communicate on time or as frequently as they promised. One father and grandfather remarked:

> What really hurts is getting a letter from a professional promising to do various things that we have requested, and then we hear nothing. They just let us down. There is nothing worse than an agency promising this, that and the other and then you never hear from them again. It makes us think, how many other people have you done this too?

In some cases, state agencies simply do not give sufficient status to families of homicide victims. I have met families who have been subjected to controlling and bullying behaviours by officials not markedly dissimilar to those used by the individuals who killed their loved ones.

Knowing the full facts of the case

After homicide, many families have enormous difficulty in achieving fundamental objectives, including satisfying a critically important need to find out the full facts of the case. In court the defendant and the state are represented by lawyers, but no one represents a victim's family.

I have seen lists produced by victim's organisations that detail what families need after homicide but they have never included the need to find out the full facts of the case. Not knowing the facts after a homicide can be extraordinarily frustrating for a family and can mean that those searching for that information will suspend almost every other activity until they get it.

> It is sobering, if not surprising, to read that bereavement through crime is so often followed by loss of employment, the breakdown of relationships and mental health problems. (Casey 2011: 3)

Helping families to acquire this information may serve at least two purposes: first, getting this information may be an important part of coping and recovering after homicide, two objectives recognised in the Government response to the consultation *Getting it right for victims and witnesses* (Ministry of Justice 2012); and second, it may save significant public resources later by avoiding the resumption of inquiries justifiably sought by families because the initial inquiry was inadequate. The families of the Hillsborough tragedy come to mind.

After Jacintha Saldanha took her own life following a hoax which led her to release medical details of a member of the Royal Family, Prime Minister David Cameron attended a select committee and was asked by Keith Vaz MP, regarding Jacintha's family: 'Do you think it is important that they be given the full facts of what happened in this case?' Mr. Cameron replied, 'Yes, of course…I think that, when these things happen, having the full facts of the case does not bring anybody back, but it does help people to come to terms with what has happened' (House of Commons 2013).

In almost every family I have met there has been a burning need to acquire details of the circumstances leading up to the homicide. But that is not always the state's objective. Budgetary pressures may cause some agencies to be satisfied with a partial understanding of the facts. For example, some homicides may present as suicides or accidents but the truth will only be revealed if agencies are willing to investigate properly. I am aware of many cases that merited a better standard of investigation. Not finding the truth may burden the victim's family with a false and hurtful narrative.

> Recommendation 1 – Government to recognise that a significant need of many families after homicide is to acquire the full facts of the circumstances leading up to the homicide.

One way, perhaps, of increasing the likelihood of the full facts being revealed to families is to equalise the advocacy power of parties at a hearing, for example, an inquest. Coroners should be able to require statutory and corporate parties to disclose the amount of funds they have made available for their legal representation at the inquest and to order that a proportion of that be awarded to the family of the deceased for their legal representation. After all, the inquest is a fact finding exercise.

> Recommendation 2 – Require statutory and corporate bodies to give a proportion of the funds they have made available for their legal representation at the inquest to the families of the deceased to pay for their own legal representation at the inquest.

It took a great deal of time and effort for my family and friends to secure the full facts surrounding the murder of my sister and nephew. This effort eventually resulted in a report that answered all of our questions (Walker et al. 2008), but it should not have taken such a gargantuan struggle to reveal the facts and, for this, we received an apology from the police. I spent a great deal of my time at work on these activities and, although I had mostly incredibly supportive managers, I often had to work long hours to keep myself employable. However, this could not last and about nine months before the review was published, I was told that my work performance would not attract a favourable appraisal. I had secured two promotions during our journey through the criminal justice system but the demands of the job were increasing and I was unable to meet them and keep my attention on both finding out the facts preceding the murders, and ensuring that I represented what I knew as accurately as possible in the domestic homicide review (Mullane

2012 cited in Monckton Smith 2012: 164), so I left under a redundancy scheme. Not all employers would treat those bereaved by homicide so favourably.

> Recommendation 3 – Statutory protection at work for those bereaved through crime, including financial assistance for small employers who might otherwise struggle to support this position in the long term.

Being integral to the domestic homicide review process

Since April 2011, domestic homicides have attracted a new type of inquiry called a domestic homicide review, under section 9 (3) of the *Domestic Violence, Crime and Victim's Act 2004*. I campaigned to ensure that a key part of these reviews offered families the opportunity to become an integral part of the inquiry. So that they were not just involved by being interviewed once or twice, perhaps, but that they influenced the scope, content and impact, were influential at the beginning, during the review process and afterwards, for example, by holding agencies to account as regards implementing improvements.

So far, as a member of the Home Office Quality Assurance Panel, I have assessed hundreds of reports from domestic homicide reviews and Advocacy After Fatal Domestic Abuse (AAFDA) has been consulted by families, other charities, local authorities or criminal justice officials on around a third of the reviews. We feel that they work best when they are exercises in humility which, in this context, means revealing the truth, being open to learning and welcoming challenge, treating the family with respect, courtesy and as key contributors, and achieving change if warranted.

A huge benefit to families is that these reviews reveal much more information about the interaction of their loved one with statutory and voluntary agencies and about interventions by others, including friends and employers, than families might have expected to have learnt from an inquest or a criminal trial. As one mother remarked:

> My other daughter usually calls me after midnight and has new questions. Having the information from the review is really helping me to answer these questions. I feel responsible for knowing the history.

Domestic homicide reviews also record a level of detail not gathered in other criminal justice processes. They are laying down a comprehensive record of the antecedents to domestic homicide and illuminating the compromised lives led by abused victims, mostly women. Further, these reviews are an opportunity for the state to learn more about domestic abuse and domestic homicide by listening to those closest to the victims and the perpetrators. Consistently after homicide, families want the voice of their loved one to be heard and they want to protect others from being harmed and killed. A problem in our justice system is that the victim's voice is largely absent (Monckton Smith 2012) so only part of the story is known. Not having the victim's perspective is empirically unsound and denies others the benefit of their experience. Too often I hear that the new willingness to allow families and friends to have a voice via domestic homicide reviews or victim personal statements, is based upon the belief that there is some cathartic value to be gained. Sometimes there is, but equally, the victim's story and the contribution of families and friends may yield the most valuable insights into why statutory and voluntary services may not be effective. And that story needs to be accurate, as one lady said after her sister was murdered:

> The victim is dead and that person is extremely dear to you. There is no more you can do to protect them but what you can do is to ensure that their story is told as accurately and truthfully as possible. You are the voice of the dead person and you have a huge responsibility to ensure their story is recorded correctly. Any deviation from that truth for me, is an injustice to the person who has died. After having read certain reports, I imagined my sister shouting 'No, no, that's not how it was. You need to get this right.' Accuracy and truth are incredibly important.

Victims of domestic abuse often tell friends, community members and their family of their difficulties long before the criminal justice system is alerted and they may only reveal certain thoughts to these people. Sometimes victims keep diaries, perhaps as a result of being told by some agencies to keep a record of the abuse. These diaries may be one of the only opportunities to represent the victim's voice directly in the criminal justice system. This input is even more important if one considers that the perpetrator often gives a less than truthful account (Adams 2007). How else will those who design and provide services really understand the lives of the deceased and the compromises they faced while trying to stay unhurt and even alive, unless they talk with those who knew them best? The reviewers are unlikely to get the full picture from agency records or the forensic narrative as told at the court trial or inquest.

> If these reviews take a broad approach, they have the potential to give a more balanced assessment of the antecedents to a killing. (Monckton Smith 2012: 5)

We should raise the status of victim accounts (both of the deceased and of family and friends), not sideline them as emotional. Many of those conducting reviews agree with this, but I am also aware of many reviews in which the involvement of families and friends has been a token exercise.

AAFDA advocates with, and on behalf of, families in these reviews, including on some technical matters, for example during discussions on publication. Those conducting the review have often remarked that our involvement has helped them too, sometimes because of our knowledge and sometimes because our peer experience has facilitated the families to place their trust in us. We have often needed to advocate for families to be given sufficient time to read the report produced by the review, before it is submitted to the Home Office for quality assurance. On one occasion, the chair of the review and a report author arrived at the family's house with a lengthy report and allowed the family two hours to read and comment on the report. This was all done as the chair and the report author sat beside them. It is very difficult to read anything while others are watching, let alone a sensitive and revealing report about one's own family. There are also the inevitable conversations that start as soon as family members start reading and any meaningful assessment becomes very difficult to achieve. We have got around this by encouraging chairs to come up with more innovative ways to give the family more time to assess these reports. In one review, the chair delivered three copies of the report on the Friday evening and then left. That evening, we spent four hours going through the report and the chair came back the following morning to hear the family's representations.

With any inquiry one of the first tasks we undertake on behalf of a family is to ask those managing it for a timeline, even if dates are indicative. Our experience is that this information is rarely volunteered or updated without a request from the family. Sometimes, those with responsibility for conducting inquiries, including coroners, will respond that they don't have fixed dates yet, but further probing will elicit that they have earmarked certain timelines within which they expect certain milestones to be achieved, for example, a pre inquest hearing or a meeting of the domestic homicide review panel. That information may be of significant value to families who may be arranging work patterns or holidays.

The extent of family involvement in domestic homicide reviews varies significantly according to a range of factors. Clearly, some may not wish to participate. I suggest another factor is the extent to which the family is informed about the process and the opportunities it provides for their contribution. A frequent lament from families is, 'If only I had known', so making informed decisions about whether or not to participate in a review may help a family avoid regrets. Another factor is the willingness of the commissioning authority and the chair of the review to seek the family's participation and to facilitate their further involvement. Participation by families in these reviews may be a journey over time rather than just a single interaction with officials. One study identified four phases to a review, including engagement with the family to input to the terms of reference (Morris et al. 2012).

Several families who were unsure about participating in domestic homicide reviews changed their minds after speaking with a representative from AAFDA. In a personal communication to me, one participant remarked:

> We were not going to get involved with the review until you helped us understand it. We are so grateful to get a second bite at the cherry.

Some families want to address the domestic homicide review panel. These panels include representatives from the statutory and voluntary agencies and they assist the chair in conducting the review. On one occasion, our request on behalf of the family was met with some concern by some panel members who felt that being at the panel meeting may upset the family and that it might inhibit how the agencies interacted at the meeting. But the chair of the review and other panel members were keen that the family should have this opportunity. It resulted in a very worthwhile meeting for the family and feedback from the panel reported that they found it a positive and enlightening experience. On another occasion, I attended a panel meeting with a family member who started crying and some of those around the table appeared a little uncomfortable. But the reality of domestic homicide is stark and it seems to me to be a good idea for professionals to witness the huge emotional toll that is caused by abuse. Having said that, given the prevalence of domestic violence, it sometimes feels unreal to talk about victims and agency workers as two discrete groups. Many of the professionals are likely to have friends or family either experiencing or perpetrating abuse and some may have suffered or be experiencing it.

Some families may not be aware that the commissioning authority, the local Community Safety Partnership, has decided not to conduct a domestic homicide review. The Home Office panel that quality assures these reviews can recommend that a review should be held but, up until August 2013, the family may not have been told that this conversation was being had. In August 2013, refreshed statutory guidance was issued and, as a result of lobbying by AAFDA, it includes a requirement for the Community Safety Partnership to 'inform the victim's family, in writing, of its position as well as any subsequent correspondence from the Quality Assurance Panel regarding its position' (Home Office 2013: 9).

To help families further with the opportunity to be integral, rather than just involved, to domestic homicide reviews we plan to initiate meetings in which the family become the interviewers of the officers providing or overseeing the various safeguarding services. So that a family's perspective permeates the whole process, consideration should also be given to inviting them to attend the Home Office meeting that quality assures the review concerning their family member.

> Recommendation 4 – Domestic homicide review practice to include opportunities for family members to interview service providers, as well as being interviewees, and to attend meetings of the Home Office panel that quality assures these reviews.

Underestimating families

'We gave it everything we could', a family told me after battling the criminal justice system just to secure their basic rights. They formed a great team after their mother/sister was killed by her husband. Their grief was immeasurable and ineffable but they had to summon up the strength to remove heavy blood stains from the house where the victim was killed. One family member said to the media, 'It's like being told – it's not your mess, but you clean it up.' Together the family channelled their extraordinary resilience and commitment into providing well thought through and skilful challenges to various bodies in the criminal justice system, now attracting interest from the highest levels.

It is often said that families of homicide victims will not be able to offer objective advice, that they will be too emotional, as if experiencing and articulating emotion was of no use and necessarily denied one's ability to think rationally. But emotion needs to be witnessed before the impact of crime can be identified, as recognised in the restorative justice process and in victim impact statements, which can affect the sentencing decisions of judges. Some families told me that, occasionally, officials expected them to be tearful at certain times, as if emotions of the bereaved should follow a script written by the state. After my sister and nephew were murdered in 2003 by her husband, my family worked for five years to uncover the full facts. At one meeting with an agency, officers seemed surprised at how organised we were, as though, perhaps, we should not have been so composed. A little bemused, we felt the need to explain that later that evening we would be lighting candles and having a good cry in private but, for now, we would be focused on the meeting for which we had thoroughly prepared. Many officials have this simplistic view of how families should seem after homicide and are surprised if they show capabilities and skills other than great emotion. However, these families were three dimensional before the killings; why wouldn't they be afterwards?

The resilience of families is often underestimated too. Understandably, officials are nervous about upsetting persons who have lost family to homicide. This is an honourable position, but it can be misplaced and slow down progress. I recently met a family in America, who agreed:

> Be ready, most survivors will want to know everything they can. If you are still uncomfortable about giving an answer that you think will be hurtful, remember what this survivor has been through already: he or she has heard that his or her daughter is dead, killed by someone who said he loved her, someone who was part of the family endured a funeral, emptied her home, and assumed responsibility for her children and pets. Believe me: if they say they can handle it, they can. Survivors, by definition, are resilient and persistent. (Bostrom 2010)

Professionals don't usually like to pick dates for meetings with the family that fall on anniversaries, perhaps of the death or the victim's birthday. However, this is an assumption and they should ask the families first. We have experience of families who felt that nothing was more fitting than to meet the agencies to try to improve the system on such a poignant day.

Inquests

Families usually have little or no knowledge of the inquest system regarding a death. It tries to elicit the answers to four questions: Who died? When? Where? How? One man, whose granddaughter was shot dead by her stalker, came to see me and lamented: 'I already know who died, when and where but I don't know how.' By which he meant under what circumstances. It is the extent of effort put into getting this answer that causes much contention at inquests.

How far a coroner will go to reveal the answer to the 'how' question may be in part informed by law, but there are other drivers. The reforms brought in on 25 July 2013 place an emphasis on coroners conducting inquests that help prevent further tragedy (Chief Coroner 2013). It seems that to do that effectively, some inquests will need to identify and evaluate the actions and inactions of agencies in the lead up to the death, that is, answer the 'how' question. This will require an understanding not only of the dynamics of domestic abuse, but also what is required of agencies that become aware of persons being domestically abused and/or stalked. How else could the coroner decide if changes were merited?

> Recommendation 5 – Coroners are offered training in understanding the dynamics of domestic abuse and stalking, including coercive control, the most dangerous form of domestic abuse. (Stark 2007)

The Ministry of Justice invited AAFDA to provide a briefing on domestic abuse for coroners in 2010 and we have recently been invited to update this briefing to include coercive control in line with the Government's new definition. I have been made aware that more than one family has been advised by the police, or another agency, that they didn't need a lawyer for the inquest as the coroner would take care of everything. Regardless of the merit of that advice, those families might have had a shock when the police and other statutory agencies arrived at the inquest represented by a barrister, perhaps a QC, paid for from the public purse. Families are frequently unaware of the extent of their rights regarding inquests and may perform passively as a result. This may suit some families, of course, but for others it may be a source of regret. Without representation from the family it is possible that coroners may not know who all the relevant witnesses are and the statutory bodies may not have or provide all the relevant evidence.

I am told that there is complex law governing this area, and I am not a lawyer, but families do need some understanding of the terms used in inquests so that they can exercise their right, as interested parties, to make representations to the coroner and so that they can understand the impact on them of the coroner's decision regarding, for example, the scope of the inquest. It may help to have some understanding of what different inquest scopes may mean, for example Article 2 European Court of Human Rights compliant *Middleton* and *Jamieson* style inquests. Significant problems may arise when families get to the end of an inquest with more questions than they had before it started, or with several questions left unanswered.

One coroner I recently had the privilege to observe appeared to conduct a very thorough investigation and supplemented it with a powerful Rule 43 statement (now called Prevention of Future Death report, which highlights issues revealed at the inquest with a view to preventing further deaths) and who left nothing to the imagination. AAFDA helped one of the families to prepare for the inquest and sat with them – as a 'McKenzie's friend' (This is an individual who assists a litigant in person. They do not need to be legally qualified) – as they prepared to ask questions of witnesses; however, by the time it was their turn, their list of questions had reduced significantly as the coroner, Mr. Andrew Tweddle, had already asked so many of them. He was persistent and forensic in his questioning of witnesses but, perhaps more importantly, he evidenced by his demeanour and follow up questions that he cared deeply that the facts were revealed. Mr. Tweddle also extended great courtesy not only to the families of the deceased but to each witness and advocate. We left feeling that a thorough job had been done and the experience, though emotional and heart-rending for the family, provided some satisfaction for them too, in large part due to the coroner's pursuit of justice and the manner in which he had conducted himself.

At one inquest, we made application to ask questions on behalf of the family as they had requested. The coroner refused and expressed a preference to hear directly from the family. The father stood up to ask the ten questions we had prepared with help from a QC, but was unable to continue after the second question due to grief. At another inquest our application to ask questions on behalf of the family was allowed. Our advocacy so far has included helping to broaden the scope of the inquest via written representations, and oral representations at the pre inquest hearing. I am hopeful that this openness to lay assistance, where families cannot afford legal help, will be allowed more often.

Recommendation 6 – In cases where families cannot afford legal help that more coroners should consider allowing lay representatives to ask questions at inquests on behalf of families. '...Munby J gave permission for a family friend to represent a mother in family proceedings. His decision confirms the law on McKenzie friends and rights of audience. Although it is a family case, the law is of wide application.' (Munby 2008)

Adjournment debates

One way for a family to influence government, shine a light on an issue and begin to lever change is via an adjournment debate. These are usually raised by backbench Members of Parliament (MPs) to bring constituents' concerns directly to government departments. The Minister is expected to attend and reply in person. They are usually set for 30 minutes but some can take much longer. Eystna Blunnie was murdered on 27 June 2012. She was pregnant at the time with her daughter Rose Louise and was due to give birth in three days. Eystna's former fiancé was found guilty of her murder and of the child destruction of Rose Louise. Eystna's parents and Rose Louise's grandparents, Kevin and Sue Blunnie, lobbied their MP, Robert Halfon, to raise an adjournment debate (House of Commons 2014). First, they wanted to raise awareness of domestic violence. Second, Mr. and Mrs. Blunnie wanted to challenge the practice of anonymity in domestic homicide reviews by having Eystna and Rose Louise's names used in the report. They wanted to highlight inconsistencies in processes, including a practice that did not allow Rose Louise to be named in the report but which, by that act, appeared to give her the status of existence when they had been unable to acquire a birth and death certificate for the unborn Rose Louise. Further, they felt that this position could not be reconciled with that of the Court's, which found Eystna's former fiancé guilty of child destruction.

Achieving change; family and friends as campaigners

Sometimes, when families want to contribute to change, we hear people remark, 'Leave it to the professionals'. That comment can send some troubling messages, including that 'the professionals' have a monopoly on useful knowledge and that only they will apply it correctly. Criminologist David Wilson, questioned whether families are in the best position to advocate for change (Wilson 2009). Some will be. Many families who experience homicide display exceptional fortitude and the extremeness of the crime sometimes gives them real clarity when identifying issues that need resolving. These qualities are a resource agencies should embrace, because a family's commitment can ensure change is implemented. It seems that, usually, it is the family of the deceased who have the stamina, persistence and drive over decades to ensure that injustices are reversed; and it is often the campaigning of friends and families which brings about some of the biggest legislative changes. Think of Stephen Lawrence's family and the Hillsborough families. These people are still having a major impact partly because, as another family commented referring to the criminal justice system agencies, 'Whilst they may forget, we don't.' This does not mean that everything a family demands should be granted. It simply means that we need to become sophisticated enough to welcome a family's views to the debate and smart enough to harness their energy and authority.

One family told me of a horrendous situation in which their name and address were publicly and loudly called out at the council offices where people were queuing for specialist help. We worked with the family to persuade a local authority to pilot a privacy card, which when presented, prompts those providing services in public areas to immediately offer the holder of the card a private space.

> Recommendation 7 – Develop the national use of privacy cards, or some other signalling process, in agencies providing public services, including job centres and council one-stop shops.

Help from those who have been bereaved through homicide

Individuals who have lost a family member to homicide and who go on to form or join organisations that help other families are often described as offering peer support. That is sometimes defined as offering emotional support, typically by spending time with the family and listening. That is a key service, but peer support also means the provision of practical and often specialist help through informing, guiding, advocating and enabling by people who have suffered similarly and who have considerable knowledge and experience. Peer led organisations often have quick access to key thinkers, other specialists, practitioners, policymakers and politicians. They are often very professionally managed and have excellent training. I have heard some senior people in the sector describe organisations that offer peer support as valuable, while they refer to those that don't as professional. It can seem as if they believe that those bereaved by homicide are precluded from offering peer support in both a valuable and a professional manner. I suggest that all individuals may have knowledge worth considering when building an understanding of problems and how to resolve them. One family member starkly described the limitations of a legal advocate:

> I don't doubt that the advocate was very busy, it was just that they could not stand in our shoes and see our overwhelming need for the truth and justice for my mum. They didn't like us asking questions and they had poor interpersonal skills. This severely affected our confidence in them and made us question their drive. They would walk away from the case and go home that day. We would live with the consequences for the rest of our lives. I don't think they saw that.

When deciding if an organisation is professional, observers might consider looking beyond the reason why it was formed to the services it provides, its knowledge base, values, training, governance, policies and practices. Many people who have lost a loved one to homicide or who have experienced crime become expert in a field they then research, but they are often referred to, primarily, as victims. There are many lawyers, social workers, politicians and other professionals who chose their careers because they witnessed an injustice often perpetrated on their own families. These people are not usually addressed as victims who happen to have a law or social work qualification, but as professionals first. Some individuals have told me that they will not reveal their personal experience of crime and how it motivated them to work in criminal justice and related sectors because they fear they will not being taken seriously. This is unfortunate because I suggest that if everyone looked around their family and close friends, it would become clear that nearly everybody's life, to some degree, has been touched by crime.

It does not follow that every family wants to speak with someone who has suffered in a similar fashion. However, a great many do in our experience in AAFDA and in the experience of other organisations in the Homicide Action Group, a forum of small to medium size organisations that provide direct services to those bereaved by homicide.

One survey of 400 families, introduced as the largest survey of bereaved families ever undertaken, revealed that 'It is hard to overplay the importance that families attach to finding others who have also been bereaved through homicide' (Casey 2011: 53). As government develops the national homicide service, it needs to consider that it should not be made up of homogenous organisations. The oft heard cry that 'we need consistency' is, I suggest, flawed thinking as this requirement may simply drive standards down to a level that most will meet. We should expect minimum standards but also embrace a rich diversity of service provision and providers as this progressive mix will continually freshen the debate and lead to a continuous improvement in the sector.

> Recommendation 8 – Government to ensure that peer led organisations receive meaningful funding in recognition of the demand for the considerable experience and knowledge they bring to families and the frequently specialist services they provide.

9
Recommendations and the Domestic Abuse First Responder Toolkit

This research has both accentuated the diverse perspectives of professionals and victims and highlighted some areas where professionals and victims agree. Frontline police officers and paramedics were very cynical about the criminal justice system and its unpredictable nature, which was a perspective shared by victims of abuse. Police officers, other frontline services and victims are variously a focus for criticism, whilst other public services can stay under the radar, even when their role in problematising domestic abuse responses is clear. For example, the knowledge of some coroners around domestic homicide has been criticised in the *Pemberton Review* (Walker et al. 2008) but there have been no significant pressures on coroners to train in this respect. Their verdicts can distort domestic abuse narratives and perceptions of the behaviour of abusers (Monckton Smith 2012). Judges and magistrates too often seem to have as much of a need for training as police officers, but there is no media campaign to make this happen. Frontline officers would probably be much less cynical if they received support from other professionals, and didn't have to rely on the victim to risk her life to help them.

There is a strong suggestion from both academics and practitioners that domestic abuse cannot be dealt with by the police alone. A clearer and better resourced care pathway for responding to abuse would include a multi-agency and community approach and a clear focus on the abuser and the victim. This may not be that difficult to achieve but it does require some recognition from professionals that they need training, that domestic abuse is not given enough status, that victims are not the problem, and that information sharing is crucial.

We have referred to a couple of high profile abuse cases that brought domestic abuse to the attention of everyone while simultaneously hiding the problem by using narratives of 'crimes of passion' or mistake. These narratives are also used by police, lawyers and coroners to rationalise domestic homicide (Monckton Smith 2012). The links between domestic abuse and domestic homicide, though well known, are extremely well hidden. Journalists' clichéd reporting of homicides is part of the problem and they need training in domestic abuse and coercive control. They too should acknowledge and talk about domestic abuse and homicide as it really is, linking cases and informing the public of the risk factors. As Stark notes, early intervention could reduce its prevalence by 70 per cent (Stark 2013). There is no earlier intervention than community support and guardianship.

In this chapter we present individual findings and related recommendations. We stress that these recommendations are not a fully formed and complete policy for future practice, but the domestic abuse toolkit (Domestic Abuse Reference Tool ©) could help give frontline officers the confidence to deal with victims and abusers, and use the system effectively. It also addresses the needs of victims, as articulated to us, in the context of a frontline response to a call for help..The contents of this toolkit address all the frustrations articulated by frontline professionals. We listened to victims, we listened to professionals and the toolkit is a practical response to everything said to us about the frontline response, and some of the criticisms put forward in the HMIC (2014) report.

> Finding 1: In a response to a call for domestic abuse, victims are chronically afraid, because of this they are strategic and recognise the limitations of the support available.

Our research has clearly highlighted some differences in the perception of domestic abuse. Police and other professionals feel frustrated with victims, whilst victims feel frustrated by the police and others. But we think that this research has highlighted an important shared frustration, which is quite hidden in the debate, about how best to respond. We have focused on the presence of police and paramedics at an emergency call for help. This is often a highly emotional situation for the victim, and not necessarily a good time to try to make decisions about her future which she may well regret soon after the police officer or paramedic leaves. Emergency response is exactly that, the practitioners are trained to manage a crisis, make sure everyone is safe for the immediate future, and deal with specialist interventions as required, like injuries or criminal offending. For police officers especially, these are the key skills of a first responder. For the most part they attend 'incidents' where these skills are required. What first responders are not particularly prepared for, or even see as their role, is ongoing involvement in the incident. This may be true for many incident types, not just domestic abuse. Police officers are used to passing on work to specialist departments, like the CID or fraud investigators, and paramedics will hand victims over to doctors in an emergency department. This probably works very well where victims are then referred on for more support or treatment, but can be more problematic when they aren't. It is also probably more effective when the judgements and actions of people in the system further down the line can be predicted. This was the purpose of domestic abuse courts, for example. But we keep hearing terrible stories that the CPS, judges, magistrates and juries are too unpredictable for victims or others to gamble on the outcome of a prosecution. There are also problems with evidence gathering at the scene to support prosecutions, police officers routinely fail to gather evidence in domestic abuse calls, which makes prosecution difficult, let alone conviction (HMIC 2014). So it is not entirely the problem that the rest of the system doesn't support the frontline, but it is a significant part. Frontline professionals have a specific job to do and domestic abuse is not always fully embraced as part of that role, for many reasons. Clear guidelines and advice at the point of first contact could help in this regard.

Similarly, when victims call for assistance, or perhaps have assistance thrust upon them when a 999 call is made by someone else, they are expecting an emergency response which keeps them safe immediately. The focus for victims is often safety, and not prosecution (Hester 2013a). They know what an emergency response is, and it does not appear that victims are expecting a long drawn out visit, but they do expect to be made safe. Thurston et al. (2009) report, from their research into screening for domestic abuse in an emergency health care community centre, that women did not always want to deal with their domestic abuse problems then and there, or disclose abuse in a screening interview or RE. They were more interested in getting the emergency dealt with; separation. for example, needs to be a considered action with proper safety planning in place. In this respect the victim of abuse recognises what the police and others can actually offer at that time. In fact, they are much better at assessing what the police and others can offer, than many professionals are. Victims often know that the police don't have the power to protect them, they frequently recognise the emergency intervention for what it is. Often they will refuse further help, because they recognise the system cannot offer safety. For a victim, the emergency response is exactly that, and further intervention would require that the police and others have a better understanding of her situation, and the tools and resources to support her properly.

In this respect, and when considered alongside the victim's strategy (Chapter 7), the most informed person in the whole equation is the victim. In many cases, it is the victim who has accurately assessed the risk (although sometimes they underestimate the seriousness, as discussed in Chapter 7). It is the victim who recognises that the police cannot offer the kind of safety they claim to be able to, it is the victim who has assessed the abuser accurately, and it is the victim who is thinking sensibly about her long term safety. Victims are acting on the resources available to them, and their assessment of when and how best to leave. Violence is not the greatest motivator for immediate action for a victim. We were told that violence is tolerated until a safe window is found for escape and that the victim's refusal to leave an abuser during a 999 call is rational. These findings were supported in the work of Pain (2013: 6) who looked at fear in domestic abuse and stated that the fear in this context was both rational and justified.

We can also see the sense in not pursuing a prosecution until the entire criminal justice system can be relied upon to support her. This includes vital evidence gathering and not just an impartial police assessment of the domestic situation. Police want her to take a punt on challenging the abuser. Her actuarial system however, is more sophisticated than theirs. Some victims may feel they can put their trust in the police or other agency, but by the following day, when that focused support is largely absent, she may well rethink her decision and reinstate her original safety plan. If police or others want women to continue with their agenda and to support a prosecution, they must remove her fear.

Recommendation: First responders should appreciate that the victim knows the limitations in the support the organisation can offer her. She may well stick to her own safety plan. A supportive and believing attitude from the professional would in fact *increase the power* of the tools available to them. If the victim felt supported, and it was genuine support, some of her fear would be removed and she may well assist the police. Professionals should be encouraged to use **validation statements** and **Rapport building** to reassure the victim (see Appendix 1.3). She may not respond at that call, but if support is consistent she may well feel safer going to the police in the future. If there is consistency, with all professionals being supportive, this gives a clear message to victim and abuser.

> Finding 2: Not all 'domestics' are the same. Professionals need to recognise the difference between an argument and abuse, and the risk of homicide.

Abuse or argument?

It became clear from our discussions with professionals that many calls for help during any kind of argument between family members were categorised under the umbrella heading of 'domestics'. The term 'domestic' brought with it a whole discourse with ready constructed discursive subjects and a backlog of police experiential 'knowledge'. A 'domestic' call is perceived as a low status drain on resources. This perception that all 'domestics' are frustrating does not differentiate between arguments and abuse. Training could give officers the skills to tell the difference, but at this time it appears that the discourse of 'domestics' predominates. Professionals need to recognise that there are arguments and there is abuse. This discrimination against domestic abuse victims has been somewhat addressed in policy by recommending that a risk assessment is performed for all domestic abuse and domestic argument calls. However, police officers do not always feel that a risk assessment is necessary and there have been moves by police services to make the risk assessment process more streamlined and focused on those who need it. Some forces have achieved this and have shortened their risk assessment forms. We appreciate that there are difficulties with a blanket risk assessment policy, in terms of time and necessity. It is not always the best time for the victim either and, where there is domestic argument rather than abuse, the risk assessment interview may be seen by the victim as unnecessary. What appears to be happening in some places is that the risk assessments are poorly performed and the forms badly completed. Sometimes a risk assessment is not done at all. There was also evidence that risk assessment forms were being completed back at the station after a shift and from memory, and in some cases by a different officer to the one who attended. The processing of these forms can also be treated with little seriousness further down the line. Those victims assessed as medium or standard risk were often left outside the system. This is not a problem if the risk assessment interview has been completed properly, but is potentially dangerous when it has not. As we have seen in this research, and noted in Chapter 5, professionals outside of the police are using screening tools in RE, for example the HITS screening tool used by paramedics in Wales and the HARK tool used by some GPs in England (Sohal et al. 2012). Similarly, Thurston et al. (2009) report using screening protocols in emergency health care settings in the USA, and Lindhorst et al. (2008) spoke of the screening process in public welfare offices. These screening tools are used in RE to encourage disclosure of abuse. Whilst the HITS acronym was the source of much criticism by paramedics because of its implied alignment with violence, there were not so many complaints about conducting the screening itself. Police officers do not use RE, and for many reasons it is not recommended, but they could screen to differentiate between abuse and argument. They have the DASH risk assessment, which can be crucial when abuse has been identified, but a blanket policy is causing problems. Pence and Sadusky (2009), who differentiate between control and abuse (battering) and other forms of domestic violence, suggest that professionals should screen for abuse and not assume all domestic violence is the same.

We found that many professionals, not just the police, often fail to differentiate between an argument and abuse. Whilst we recognise that police officers do not practice RE, they might still find it helpful to have a screening tool to help them recognise abuse. It may help police officers to carry an aide memoire/screening tool in their domestic abuse toolkit so that they can use research and evidence to recognise where a risk assessment interview is necessary or advisable. We do not suggest that this recommendation is taken without serious consideration, similarly we do not suggest that the five questions we offer are anything other than suggestions, which could be further discussed by experts in the field; we also suggest that the screening tool is just *part* of a domestic abuse toolkit for professionals.

Ellen Pence, who developed the power and control wheel, advises that everything in domestic abuse is about context and she presents three questions to differentiate domestic arguing and fighting from abuse or battering:

1. Is this action part of an ongoing pattern of behaviour?
2. Is this pattern of behaviour intended to instil fear?
3. Is this pattern of behaviour linked to domination and control?

Pence and Sadusky (2009)

Recommendation: an aide memoire/screening tool could be used to help officers differentiate between arguments and abuse, and to identify CONTROL. This tool could include, for example, five high risk factors for abuse which indicate control is being used. If even one of these factors is present, the context questions should be considered and a risk assessment should then be performed as soon as practicable, or if this is not possible the victim should be designated enough risk status for referral to further support. The questions we would recommend including and follow the acronym FEARS for reference are:

Frightened – is the victim very frightened?

Estrangement or its threat – has there been a separation or is it threatened?

Aggression, Control and Violence – is there disclosure of aggression, control or violence happening at any time?

Repeat abuser – has the alleged perpetrator got a history of abuse, in this or any other relationship?

Stalking/harassment – is there any stalking or harassment occurring?

Context:

Is this incident part of ongoing behaviour?

Is it intended to instil fear?

Is it linked to control?

Pence and Sadusky (2009)

Risk of homicide

Once abuse is identified, or if officers already knew of abuse, they could look at the key questions that can help predict homicide risk in very dangerous men. Snider et al. (2009) conducted research in the USA to determine which assessment questions were the most useful in determining risk for future serious injury or homicide. They identified five questions, which could be asked in a healthcare setting, to screen for possible homicide. If the woman answered yes to three out of five questions, she could be considered high risk for homicide or serious violence. Those five questions are:

1. Has the physical violence increased in frequency or severity over the last six months?
2. Has he ever used a weapon or threatened you with a weapon?
3. Do you believe he is capable of killing you?
4. Have you ever been beaten by him while you were pregnant?
5. Is he violently and constantly jealous of you?

This research was based on women who had gone to an emergency department for treatment for an injury from their abusive partner. These women will be a slightly different profile to those women who are not beaten, or who do not seek help for their injuries. Campbell (2014) argues that there is nearly always prior physical or sexual violence (actual or threatened) in high risk abusive relationships. But suggests that if it is established then, based on the research, the following questions would suggest a high risk situation:

Screening for homicide risk:

1. Has he threatened to kill you or your children?
2. Has he used a weapon against you or threatened you with a weapon?
3. Has there been a separation?
4. Is he unemployed?
5. Do you have a child that is not his?
6. Does he control most or all of your daily activities?
7. Does he force you into sex?
8. Does he choke you?
9. Does he hit you while you are pregnant?

> Finding 3: Recognising vulnerable, intimidated and repeat victims was difficult for professionals: these victims were more likely to be given the least service. (Hester 2013a, Stark 2013)

There is much talk about domestic abuse victims being considered as repeat victims, but less acceptance that they are vulnerable and intimidated. Whilst we have witnessed difficulties with professionals defining what constitutes a repeat victim, at least they are recognising the importance of that status. All professionals should consider a woman a repeat victim if she discloses that she is such. Relying on calls for help as evidence of repeat victimisation is not enough, especially if we consider that most women will have been assaulted many times before they call for assistance. Domestic abuse victims suffer from ongoing control and everyday terrorism (Pain 2014), not only is it repeated but it is intimidating. When women refuse to take medical or criminal justice help it is often because of intimidation. The victim's code states that victims who are intimidated, and that specifically means too afraid to follow a prosecution, should be considered intimidated and must therefore receive an *enhanced service*. Often, police do not follow their options to pursue prosecutions for witness intimidation or even consider that the victim is intimidated. They are quicker to believe she is reckless or frustrating. Chronically frightened victims are often in need of more support, they may be suffering with a mental health disturbance, substance abuse, alcohol abuse or anger and agitation.

The effects of chronic fear should not be underestimated. Some professionals consider that name calling is psychological abuse, they do not have in their skill repertoire the knowledge of chronic fear brought about through coercive control. Consequently, many repeat, vulnerable and intimidated victims are treated as time wasters, or as creators of their own problems. When chronic fear is made worse by a lack of support from those who may be the last hope for support, the effects can be catastrophic for the victim. And, from a police perspective, if she is not supported she will never make a statement for prosecution, and may even end up dead. It is crucial that first responders are supportive and *believe* in her fear and distress. Sohal et al. (2012) describe a series of validation statements which could be used to assure victims who have disclosed abuse. A similar set of statements could be included in the toolkit, along with suggestions for asking difficult questions. As with any interview or conversation, a period of rapport building should come first, and this is especially the case where a difficult subject is to be tackled, like child sexual abuse (Fogarty et al. 2013), as discussed in Chapter 5. Professionals should feel comfortable speaking with victims and asking them questions in a caring manner, which may begin to encourage them to talk, for example:

> How are things at home?
> Are you happy?
> Are you frightened?

Validation statements cited by Sohal et al. (2012)

Everybody deserves to feel safe at home.

You don't deserve to be hit or hurt. It is not your fault.
I am concerned about your safety and wellbeing.
You are not alone. Help is available.
You are not to blame. Abuse is common and happens in all kinds of relationships. It tends to continue.
Abuse can affect your health and that of your children in many ways.

Recommendation: In the domestic abuse toolkit for first responders there should be validation statements to help them deal appropriately with chronically afraid victims and some suggestions for rapport building questions. Validation statements and rapport building questions should ideally be used in private. Other professionals, like GPs, use these tools and it is not patronising but helpful to have an example of the kind of thing to say.

Finding 4: Police officers often fail to identify, or respond to, the offences being committed. The more offences recognised, the more chances of successful prosecution.

There have been moves to make charging easier and to include charges to capture the whole incident in one. However, there has been some research from America which suggests that prosecutions are more successful where there are multiple charges on the sheet. They found that where there were four charges the conviction rate was 100 per cent, whereas one charge attracted only a 29 per cent conviction rate (Lonsway 2006). It is also suggested that most (over 95 per cent) of cases were cleared through plea bargaining. This may be more easily achieved with multiple charges. Early observation and taking notes of victim statements and offender behaviours, may strengthen future prosecutions. First responders should be aware of the situation they are observing and begin to take seriously, and recognise, intimidation and harassment. We found that these two particular offences are routinely overlooked in domestic abuse;. many other offences are often committed, like criminal damage, threats to kill, assault, witness intimidation harassment and so on. Research suggests that there should be aggressive prosecution policies in respect of domestic abuse (Stark 2013). HMIC (2014) found that many police officers are failing to collect evidence properly, and in a snapshot file review they found that in 600 cases of actual bodily harm (ABH) photographs were taken in only half the cases, and statements did not include the basic details of description of injuries or the scene. In Recommendation 10 we have included suggestions for evidence gathering in strangulation assault, which give a general feel for the professionalism and skill required to aid prosecution, and for police officers to garner some support, and perhaps trust, in the predictability of the system ahead. There is also an evidence gathering guide in the developed toolkit (DART ©)

Recommendation: Once first responders have identified domestic abuse they should begin to start gathering evidence for a number of offences which may be being committed, including harassment, threats to kill, and witness intimidation. Put multiple charges on the charge sheet. And *recognise that a number of offences are often being committed.*

Professionals should begin and continue the investigation assuming the victim will not support the prosecution. There may be other evidence. The more it is about other evidence rather than 'she said, he said', the more likely the prosecution will succeed, and the more likely she will be to support it. Taking photographs, and use of body video wear. may also assist a victimless prosecution.

> Finding 5: Abusers are too often absent from discussions about their behaviour, and the problems they are causing. Police officers and other professionals see domestic abuse as a 'female' problem, created by females into which men get drawn. The abusers are often just responding as 'men' to female problematic behaviour.

Abusers should not be considered as 'ordinary blokes' who just lost control. These men may be suffering from various dysfunctions that place them on a psychopathic or psychotic spectrum; equally, they may be unable to deal with rejection or other life challenges for many societal, cultural and socio-structural reasons; they may have depression or other mental health issues, attachment disorders or substance abuse problems.

It has been suggested that any man could be an abuser, but we should consider that this is what has kept alive and acceptable the excuses and justifications that diminish the seriousness of abuse. Domestic killers are an identifiable group, their killings can often be predicted (Adams 2007). One of the criticisms is that not all abusers will end up killing, and this is true, but their potential to do so remains until they are challenged, treated or rehabilitated. It is also the case that even if they don't kill, their actions are a massive cost to society, in both human and financial terms. This isn't retrospection, the risk assessment tools) and what we know about coercive control can proactively help predict high risk and dangerousness in many cases. We discussed the case of Mick Philpott in Chapter 1, a man treated as if he was a bit of a rogue rather than an abuser. His neighbours perceived his violence and control as an extreme of normal masculine behaviour, despite his conviction for stabbing a former girlfriend. This man was not 'normal', he displayed characteristics of psychopathy and narcissism and was unable to deal with challenge or rejection. The problems with pathologising personality or mental health notwithstanding, Mick Philpott displayed many of the high risk behaviours for homicide, as did OJ Simpson and Raoul Moat. In this respect, men displaying those behaviours should be 'profiled' by professionals,and responded to with whatever tools the system makes available. More work should be done in constructing models for understanding domestic killers, to raise the status of this form of homicide. Domestic abuse is not all about victim care and difficult sensitivities, any more than other forms of violence or terrorism, like stranger killings, which give the victim and the violence more status. Domestic abuse is not for the fainthearted, it's ugly, dangerous and difficult. We need to start taking domestic abusers seriously and treating them like the dangerous people they are; the way we treat other categories of dangerous individuals and potential killers.

We suggest that a 'profiling tool' or risk interview is developed, much like the screening tool, to help officers quickly recognise high risk abusers and remember that there are more dangerous behaviours than violence. For example, the evidence that control predicts homicide better than violence by a ratio of 9:1 is not well known (Stark 2009) and professionals still adhere to the belief that violence is the best, or even only, predictor of dangerousness. Not only would such a tool remind officers of dangerous behaviours, it could also form the basis for a conversation to address abusive behaviour between the professional and the abuser. Police officers and other professionals told us that they felt as uncomfortable talking to abusers, as they did talking to victims, unless they could talk to them in the context of their professional role; for example, if the abuser was to be arrested police were more confident, and paramedics were more confident where the abuser was injured. At this time most conversations appear to revolve around getting the victim to support a prosecution, or managing the situation so that it appears safe enough for the professionals to leave. A conversation addressing the abuser's potentially criminal behaviour, with some advice for where that might lead, at least acknowledges the abuser as the problem. Research has acknowledged for many years that abuse continues because it is tacitly accepted. Challenging abusers would remove his certainty in solidarity or support for his abuse. This also relates to Recommendation 12, which suggests interagency training is shown to increase a professional's confidence in talking to victims and taking action in domestic abuse calls.

Consistency is essential. Professionals in all organisations should give the message that domestic abuse is wrong and will not be tolerated. When an abuser acknowledges their behaviour or discloses abuse professionals should:

1. Acknowledge that domestic abuse is wrong. Be consistent. Domestic abuse is a crime.
2. Acknowledge this is the first step to addressing the problem.
3. Affirm behaviour. Remind them their behaviour is a choice and they can stop.
4. Be respectful, but do not show solidarity. Domestic abuse is a crime.
5. Offer a helpline number (CAADA recommend RESPECT or a local helpline).
6. Be aware that abusers minimise and deny.

(adapted from CAADA 2014)

Recommendation: Abusers should be profiled by first responders and not treated as if they were ordinary men having an argument with their wife. A history from the victim, and observation of the behaviour of the alleged abuser, can often allow a first responder to recognise risk. A profiling/risk interview tool with the highest risk behaviours may alert officers to any dangers and be a guide for a conversation about criminal behaviour. We suggest the following could be potential high risk behaviours – these are suggestions only, – framed as questions to indicate whether he is empathetic: These should not be used as a set of questions posed directly to the abuser, but as a set of reminders for the professional to help them with their professional judgement:

Has this person ever threatened to commit suicide or made threats to kill?

Does this person have a history of abuse or violence in this or any other relationship?

Does this person use weapons?

Is there a separation or is a separation threatened?

Has there ever been an accusation of a strangulation assault?

How happy is this person for the victim to leave?

Is this person accused of harassment or stalking?

How genuinely emotional is he right now?

Does he talk about himself and his perspective?

Does he think the current incident is serious?

Does he feel he is to blame for this current incident?

Is he willing to get help?

Context: is he manipulative?

Is this part of ongoing control?

Finding 6: Often, men will not recognise that they are abusive until they see their behaviour through someone else's eyes. However, some do recognise their abuse. Some men self-refer for support, and some abusers have disclosed to us in training sessions and become quite distressed, wanting to access help. Some abusers do not see they are doing anything wrong.

Abusers are not the focus for much attention apart from arrest. All alleged abusers should be shown an abuser profile so that they can recognise their own abuse. Abusers are a heterogeneous group, but they share some behavioural characteristics. Whatever the reason for their abuse, it is still dangerous behaviour for him and anyone he is abusing. These behaviours should not be treated as 'normal', and the excuse of *crime of passion* should be dismissed. Abusers exert ongoing control, they do not suddenly kill someone out of nowhere, as some media reporters and criminal justice professionals would have us believe (Monckton Smith 2012). Some men want help, some can be made aware of the fact that their behaviour won't be tolerated and may be deterred, some men know they are abusive and have every intention of continuing. Whatever the response, the abuser could be given a roadmap to show where his abuse might lead, accentuating the negatives for him. We suggest a card with a self-completion questionnaire on the front and a road map on the back. The abuser could be asked to consider the self-completion questions. in a police car or cell if arrested, or in his own time if removed from the home, or he could be left with the card if he was allowed to stay. The self-completion questionnaire is for his information only. It is not to be shown to anyone else, the officer does not have to know the answers. It may be that he throws it away, but that's no reason not to give it to him, and to keep giving it to him. There was some evidence from Jewell and Wormith (2010) that abusers can use perpetrator programme material to abuse the victim further, though this didn't appear to be a widespread action. There is a possibility that the abuser would be incensed at being given an abuse roadmap, or being told to leave the premises, or being arrested. The roadmap lets him know he's on the radar. Some abusers do not see that their behaviour is wrong or unacceptable. Some feel that they have every right to carry on, and the permission of their communities to do so. Society, criminal justice and media still do not denounce them enough so abusers feel they have some solidarity with the culture and their peers (Monckton Smith 2012, Dawson 2003, Lees 1997). We have talked about how solidarity with the abuser is shown in many cases. This is starkly shown in the case studies of Raoul Moat, OJ Simpson and Elliot Turner. There needs to be a reminder that the solidarity is no longer there. The road map should be shown as the abuser's future.

Recommendation: Abusers could be shown an abuser profile with a roadmap to help and support, and a warning of the possibility of homicide, the criminal justice sanctions available and what that would mean for them. This profile could include a self-completion questionnaire to make him aware of how his behaviour might be considered abusive. These questions are just suggestions:

Are you jealous?

Do you try to control your partner's behaviour, money, time and so on?

Do you expect total devotion and commitment from your partner?

Do you expect your partner to be able to do everything you want her to

Do you feel better when no one else is around her, like her family and friends?

Do you check her phone?

Is she to blame for how you feel, like when you get angry or upset?

Do you expect her to have sex when you want to, even if she is ill or asleep, or unwilling?

Do you say nasty things to her?

Do you think women and men are different?

Can your partner go out with who she likes when she likes?

Do you stop her from making her own decisions?

Do you hit or assault her?

Do you have control of her money?

Do you follow her or check on her movements?

Abuse roadmap: this could happen if you don't stop

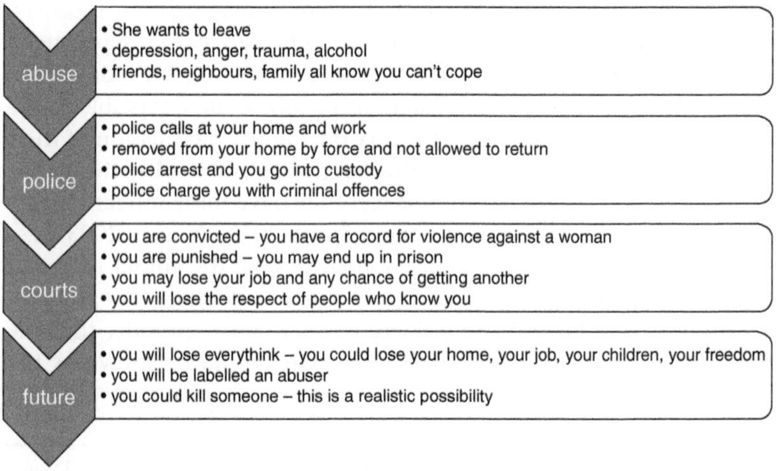

abuse
- She wants to leave
- depression, anger, trauma, alcohol
- friends, neighbours, family all know you can't cope

police
- police calls at your home and work
- removed from your home by force and not allowed to return
- police arrest and you go into custody
- police charge you with criminal offences

courts
- you are convicted – you have a rocord for violence against a woman
- you are punished – you may end up in prison
- you may lose your job and any chance of getting another
- you will lose the respect of people who know you

future
- you will lose everythink – you could lose your home, your job, your children, your freedom
- you will be labelled an abuser
- you could kill someone – this is a realistic possibility

Domestic abuse is not acceptable, you must stop now

Abuse is not just violence, abuse is about control. If you feel you need help to deal with depression, anger, alcohol or substance abuse, or other issues affecting your behaviour, you might want to consider getting some help before things get worse. There is information on this card to help you do this.

If you are abusive the police will get involved, as society does not accept this kind of behaviour.

There are many offences you could be convicted of : assault, threats to kill, harassment and stalking, witness intimidation, criminal damage, theft, and many more.
Stop and think.
THE POLICE WILL PROSECUTE YOU.
Abuse will escalate and you will lose everything if you don't stop.
Get help.
Numbers....

Finding 7: Professionals do not always recognise, or even know about, coercive control, despite its importance in assessing risk and its presence in the official definition for domestic abuse.

Coercive control is a course of conduct and is the most common form of abuse perpetrated against women by abusive men. The methods and behaviours are not well, or consistently, recognised in any part of society or professional practice, except specialist women's abuse services. If the abuse is not severe and there is no assault, it can be mistakenly assumed that it's not serious. This could not be further from the truth. Women who suffer low level assaults and are controlled, are in just as much, if not more, danger than those women who are more severely injured. He is not scared, he is in control and he may be able to behave in a rational manner, but this will not always be the case – he may well be angry or frustrated – this should not be treated as 'her' being the problem. Hester (2013a) and Stark (2013) suggest that the victims who most need support and help are those who routinely do not get it. Substance abuse and alcohol addiction, for example, are highly likely where a victim is controlled or abused. This should be recognised by officers and paramedics. Alcohol does not *cause* domestic abuse, it can certainly make matters worse. It is also probable that a victim may display mental health disturbance, this is not unusual for victims who are suffering from chronic fear (Pain 2014). Coercion and control are now included in the official definition for domestic abuse and are the most dangerous behaviours. The language of 'psychological abuse' does not always capture the chronic fear brought about by coercive control (Stark 2007) or everyday terrorism (Pain 2014).

Recommendation: Repeat calls for help from women suffering low level assaults may mean they are actually suffering severe control. Instead of being frustrated with her, remember you may be her only lifeline, do not give up on her. Use the **screening questions** (see Appendix 1.1) to help recognise if this is abuse, use the **validation statements** (Appendix 1.3) to gain trust, and perform a formal risk assessment where possible. Do not be fooled into thinking that he is plausible, complete an **abuser profile/risk interview** (Appendix 1.4) and give him the **roadmap** (Appendix 1.7). If she has confidence in you she may help you to help her. Chronic fear brought about by coercive control is serious.

> Finding 8: Violence which is not severe is not treated as serious (Stark 2013) and police officers are advising victims there is nothing they can do, often telling victims that they need to witness something serious before they will act.

Stark (2013) states that early intervention in domestic abuse could reduce its prevalence by 70 per cent. Victims are routinely told that the situation isn't serious enough to warrant intervention. They report that police tell them they need to be assaulted before they can do anything, or they have to wait for a criminal offence to occur. Robust intervention in the earlier stages is argued as effective in reducing its prevalence. This is partly because of the low status of domestic abuse and its victims, where non-serious assault compounds the perceived trivial nature of the complaint. However, much coercive control does not reach the level of criminality and many abusers rely on this. We have already discussed that officers should recognise that multiple offences may be being committed and they should consider more than violence or assault. Even where they cannot identify offending they should have a risk interview with the alleged abuser and a conversation about the abuser profile and offending pathway. Don't wait for the abuse to escalate before intervening.

Recommendation: Deal robustly with early complaints of abuse. Women should be believed and **validation statements** (Appendix 1.3) used; abusers should be given a **risk interview** (Appendix 1.4) **and self completion questionnaire** (Appendix 1.6), and left with a **roadmap** (Appendix 1.7) showing: the pathway of offending and where it will lead; the help that is available; a warning about their behaviour. This information, and the warning, should be recorded against the abuser's name on a domestic abuse database.

> Finding 9: Professionals do not always recognise risk for a potential homicide, and even where they do they throw their hands in the air and declare that it's the victim's fault if she gets killed, because she didn't leave. They do not always recognise that a domestic abuse call where there is coercive control, is potentially their chance to actually prevent a homicide. They sometimes fail to see these calls as

> real police work; they are probably the most real police work many officers will experience, bringing them closer to a killer than they are likely to be anywhere else.

It seems from our research that professionals approach domestic abuse calls as unimportant and not really their job to deal with. The fact is that dealing with an abuse call could be the closest many officers get to preventing a homicide. This really IS their work. This is dealing with a potential killer, and statistically this is the call where they are most likely to meet a killer, and in the context where he is likely to kill. This is not an abstract possibility. This could end with a death. This is probably one of the more serious and more challenging police problems. Police officers should recognise the serious nature of abuse, control and chronic fear.

Recommendation: Treat every domestic abuse call, where there is control, as a potentially very serious and dangerous situation. This is the kind of call where professionals could really prevent the most serious violence on our statute books – homicide. Use the domestic abuse toolkit road map, offender profile/risk interview, and validation statements. Look for offending and be alert in collecting evidence. Consider the high risk characteristics and speak with the victim in a manner which will gain her trust. Use validation statements in private and build rapport.

> Finding 10: Strangulation assault has been acknowledged as very high risk for future homicide. From our research we have found that these assaults are not taken seriously, even where victims have lost consciousness.

Certain violence is more dangerous than others, not just in the sense that it is more likely to cause death or serious injury, but in what it predicts. Research studies have shown that any kind of strangulation assault is dangerous and highly predictive of future homicide (Schwartz 2010). A large number of states in America, including New York and Minnesota, have upgraded strangulation assault to felony status because too many of these assaults were being routinely recorded as misdemeanours (less serious assaults), which did not reflect its seriousness. In the UK, it seems from our research, strangulation assault is quite often ignored, or offenders are just cautioned. In some cases risk assessments aren't even done where a woman has been strangled to unconsciousness, or this kind of strangulation is attributed to 'sex games'. Strangulation, or simulated strangulation, should always be considered dangerous, it is high risk for, and predicts, future homicide. Volochinsky (2012) states that strangulation assault is treated like it was a slap in the face. Quite often strangulation can leave no visible injuries, despite the serious injury and trauma it can cause. The clinical sequence for strangulation is severe pain, followed by unconsciousness, followed by brain death (Volochinsky 2012). Strangulation is a powerful symbolic act of control, and a very real and visceral threat to life. When an abuser puts his hands on the victim's neck and squeezes he has indicated his intention to kill (Volochinsky 2012). During a strangulation assault victims will feel they are being killed, this may create significant and long lasting fear, chronic fear. Better training in gaining evidence for strangulation assault is indicated, especially in emergency departments, coupled with good evidence gathering by the police. The evidence of strangulation which can be noted may be:

- Voice changes (hoarseness, raspy voice, or loss of voice)
- Swallowing changes (difficulty or pain)
- Breathing changes (difficulty or inability to breathe)
- Involuntary incontinence
- Miscarriage
- Mental status changes (sleep disturbance, amnesia, stress, restlessness or combativeness)
- Nausea or dizziness
- Scratches/fingernail marks, scrapes, and abrasions (from offender or defensive injuries)
- Redness, swelling, abrasions, or bruising on the neck
- Petechiae (tiny ruptured capillaries that look like red spots) on eyes, face or neck
- Ligature marks
- Broken/fractured bones or injured cartilage in the neck
- Lung damage, fluid in the lungs, or pneumonia
- Brain injury caused by lack of oxygen
- Vision or hearing changes
- Memory loss

(Schwartz 2010)

Other evidence which may be gathered to aggressively pursue an assault charge, as noted by Schwartz (2010), is listed below. The list is a model for evidence gathering practices more generally to make sure that domestic abuse is treated seriously, that abusers can see they are being treated as criminals, and that the future outcome of the case can be better predicted. Victims witnessing such professional activity and support may well be more likely to support a prosecution:

- Take photographs of the victim's injuries and red marks, no matter how minor. Remember that some physical injuries may become apparent or visible as many as several days after an incident, so swelling, marks and bruises should be repeatedly photographed to show their evolution over time. Note: some of the victim's injuries (i.e., scratches or fingernail marks) may be 'self-inflicted' where the victim is struggling to stop the offender's manual strangulation or to remove a ligature from around the throat, neck, mouth or nose.
- If the area where the strangulation took place shows evidence of a struggle (i.e., broken furniture, holes in the walls, tousled blankets), take documentary photographs or video.
- If a ligature was used, try to locate and secure that object.
- If the offender's hands, arms, knees, or other body parts were used to strangle, have the victim recount the details.
- If the offender had marks or injuries on her/his body (i.e., bite marks on hands, scratches on arms or hands) characterise these injuries as defensive if they are consistent with the victim's report of a struggle.
- Encourage the victim to recall words the offender used during the attack that indicated an intent to injure, strangle, or kill.
- Encourage the victim torecount what thoughts were going through her/his mind during the incident (*did the victim fear death; was there resignation that death or serious injury was imminent?)*
- Encourage the victim to try and recall how long she/he perceived the strangulation to last and how much pressure/strength of grip the offender used.
- Interview witnesses such as neighbours, paramedics, GP and so on.
- Use 999 call records, as these may contain evidence of the victim's voice horseness or raspiness, hyperventilation, fear and more, during or after the incident.
- Audio-record the victim's voice to document voice changes.
- Encourage the victim to recount injuries received during and after the incident, such as difficulty breathing, swallowing, neck or throat pain, voice changes, or nausea.
- Try to get the victim to recount episodes of numbness, dizziness, faintness, or loss of consciousness, during or after the incident.
- Did the victim involuntarily defecate or urinate during the attack? If so, did the victim change clothes before seeking help or medical assistance? Note that victims may be extremely embarrassed about

discussing these particular details, but assure the victim they are medically consistent with the crime suffered.

- Include any previous strangulation incidents perpetrated by this offender in the victim statement.
- The victim should describe prior acts of domestic abuse or violence, as well as any threats to injure or kill.
- Utilise a medical expert to testify about the risk associated with strangulation and the nature of strangulation-related injuries. Schwartz (2010)

Recommendation: Any type of strangulation assault should be taken very seriously. Strangulation or simulated strangulation comes before homicide. Any man using this type of violence should be charged with assault, and not receive a caution, and certainly not NFA (No Further Action). Where there is a history (disclosed by the victim) of abuse or control the sex game argument should be dismissed immediately. A formal risk assessment must always be carried out for strangulation assault, and *high risk* status should always be *considered*. If there is a history of abuse, this victim should be considered high risk, irrespective of the answers to the other questions. Strong and meticulous evidence gathering should begin immediately

Finding 11: We found that stalking and harassment is seen as non-serious, despite being one of the biggest predictors of homicide along with history of abuse:

In cases where a partner or former partner is harassing or stalking the victim, this is highly suggestive of high risk. Officers taking such calls should consider all offences that are being committed, and place them in the context of domestic abuse. Too often criminal damage or theft will not be recorded as domestic abuse, when this offending is in the context of stalking or control. The riskiest cluster of stalking behaviours are: following to work or school; damage to property; leaving abusive messages (Campbell et al. 2007). Research considers stalking of a former or current intimate partner as the most dangerous form of stalking, and the most likely to continue for a long time. It is also considered the form of stalking most resilient to intervention:

Recommendation: Where a victim complains of stalking this is abuse and a high risk behaviour. A risk assessment should be done. There should be a stalking aide memoire in the domestic abuse toolkit. There is new legislation to respond to stalking because it is a highly dangerous behaviour. The following cluster is considered dangerous and would be included on the stalking aide memoire, along with other high risk stalking behaviours:

Cluster of three: following to work or school; leaving abusive messages; damage to property.

Also: prior abuse; control or violence; prior sexual assault.

Stalking is repeated and persistent, harassment takes many forms: is the victim frightened?

Finding 12: Interagency or inter-professional training would give professionals more confidence to deal with domestic abuse and is wanted by professionals.

There have been great moves in developing multi-agency hubs in public protection and domestic abuse so that communication between agencies is made more efficient and easier. Information sharing is often raised as an area in need of improvement, and professionals themselves raised this as an issue. The hubs appear to be working in a case management context. It would be beneficial, however, if this ethos was developed in the training context. We have found that training is largely delivered by people who are trained in how to train, rather than being experts in any particular area. This means that police officers, for example, are being trained with and by other police officers. This does not expand their perception of the 'problem' they are presented with. It is looked at from a police perspective, and police discursive knowledge, only. Sometimes victims have some contact in a training session, but this appears to be the only other perspective presented. Sharing training in domestic abuse, where multiple agencies are involved and could offer support, could be beneficial in many ways. Research has suggested that interagency and inter-professional training gives professionals more confidence in dealing with victims and taking action (Szilassy et al. 2014). It has been found that professionals do not feel they want to deal with domestic abuse, but that knowing what other help is available and knowing the full care pathway gives them the confidence to approach the victim and take action. It has been suggested many times that an organisation's culture can be a bar to improving services, inter-professional training, especially in case study work, may help break the power of a cultural bias.

Recommendation: Police officers, paramedics and other support staff and agencies should organise regular joint training days where they learn about each other's agendas and processes, and share knowledge and experience. Multi-agency teams should work on case study material to show clearly where they can all fit in and where support is available for both the victim and the professional. This type of interaction should also be used to improve future professional relationships and form supportive practices.

Concluding comments

We have presented some recommendations for frontline responses to domestic abuse. These suggestions for *framing practice* are based on the comments made to us by professionals and victims and we hope they align expectations in many ways. Where professionals recognise serious abuse they do take it seriously, but what is serious is not always recognised. Also, domestic abuse, where it is recognised as serious, carries with it a new set of concerns for the professional. Can they respond properly? Do they have the confidence to respond? What should they say? Will they make it worse? They want more power to respond to abusers. We hope that we have also addressed these concerns in some small part. The toolkit should help first responders and professionals understand and respond confidently to a call for help. It does not offer all the answers, and it would benefit from further discussion and debate. Multi or interagency training is not part of the toolkit itself, but would support the information it provides. The toolkit does not seek to replace existing tools in frontline use. It is a set of guidance and reference cards, and some information to hand to abusers, which may help structure a response. It could also be used in training to structure good practice and to answer some of the concerns of professionals.

The toolkit is meant predominantly to respond to professional and victim frustrations, the material in it seeks to raise the status of the abuse and the victim and her strategy, and therefore improve the response to her. Much more work is required to raise the status of abuse and its victims in more general terms and the co-operation of the whole criminal justice system, the health system, local government, national government, media of all forms, the education system and communities is required. The dominant discourse is being resisted and a clear care pathway for victims, and intervention pathway for abusers, would create easier partnership working and co-operation and give everyone more confidence in the system, and start to erode the dominance and power of the domestic abuse myths. When the myths are challenged, the status of the abuse, and the victims can start to rise.

The skeleton toolkit presented in this chapter and in the appendices has been developed as a training and operational aide for all professionals responding to domestic abuse. For further information please contact the author Dr Jane Monckton Smith: jmoncktonsmith@glos.ac.uk

Appendix 1: Domestic Abuse First Responder Toolkit

Author's note: Domestic Abuse Reference Tool © Jane Monckton Smith

The findings of the research discussed in this book were organised to form a toolkit for professionals from any agency which may come into contact with victims of domestic abuse. A skeleton version of this toolkit is presented in Chapter 9, and the appendices. The professional version has been developed and piloted, and is now available for multi-agency use.

For further information please contact the author Dr Jane Monckton Smith: jmoncktonsmith@glos.ac.uk

Suggested screening tool to differentiate abuse and argument:

Appendix 1.1

Is this domestic abuse? Some help and/or professional judgement should be used.

Frightened – is the victim very frightened?

Estrangement or its threat – has there been a separation or is it threatened?

Aggression, Control and Violence – is there disclosure of aggression, control or violence happening at any time?

Repeat abuser – has the alleged perpetrator got a history of abuse in this or any other relationship?

Stalking/harassment – is there any stalking or harassment occurring?

Context:

Is this incident part of ongoing behaviour?

Is it intended to instil fear?

Is it linked to control?

Pence and Sadusky (2009)

High risk behaviours – risk of homicide

Appendix 1.2

High risk behaviours which raise the risk for homicide. Ask:

1. Has this person threatened to kill you or your children?
2. Have they used a weapon against you or threatened you with a weapon?
3. Has there been a separation?
4. Is this (abuser) unemployed?
5. Do you have a child that is not his?
6. Does this person control most or all of your daily activities?
7. Does he force you into sex?
8. Does he choke/strangle you?
9. Has he hit you while you are pregnant?

If the first two are present then this is high risk. The presence of the other factors raises the risk, or can signify risk. Use your professional judgement.

Validation statements – for consistency and support

Appendix 1.3

Example validation and rapport building statements:

How are things at home?
Are you happy?
Are you frightened?

Validation statements cited by Sohal et al. (2012)
Everybody deserves to feel safe at home.
You don't deserve to be hit or hurt. It is not your fault.
I am concerned about your safety and wellbeing.
You are not alone. Help is available.
You are not to blame. Abuse is common and happens in all kinds of relationships. It tends to continue.
Abuse can affect your health and that of your children in many ways.

Abuser profiling/risk interview

Appendix 1.4

Abuser profile/risk These are some example questions which may indicate whether this person is an abuser. They may be helpful where the victim is unable or unwilling to speak with you or if you want to assess the risk of this person:

Has this person ever threatened to commit suicide or made threats to kill?
Does this person have a history of abuse or violence in this or any other relationship?
Does this person use weapons?
Is there a separation or is a separation threatened?
Has there ever been an accusation of a strangulation assault?
How happy is this person for the victim to leave?
Is this person accused of harassment or stalking?
How genuinely emotional is he right now?
Does he talk about himself and his perspective?
Does he think the current incident is serious?
Does he feel he is to blame for this current incident?
Is he willing to get help?
Context: is he manipulative?
Is this part of ongoing control?

Where abuse is disclosed by the abuser:

Appendix 1.5

Has someone disclosed to you that they are an abuser?

1. Acknowledge that domestic abuse is wrong. Be consistent. Domestic abuse is a crime.
2. Acknowledge this is the first step to addressing the problem.
3. Affirm any behaviour. Remind them their behaviour is a choice and they can stop.
4. Be respectful, but do not show solidarity. Domestic abuse is a crime. Be consistent.
5. Offer a helpline number (CAADA recommend RESPECT or a local helpline).
6. Be aware that abusers minimise and deny

(adapted from CAADA 2014)

Helpline number...

Abuser self-completion card

Appendix 1.6

If you answer yes to even one or two of these questions you could be guilty of domestic abuse.

Are you really jealous?
Do you try to control your partner's behaviour, money, time and so on?
Do you expect total devotion and commitment from your partner?
Do you expect your partner to be able to do everything you want her to do?
Do you feel better when no one else is around her, like her family and friends?

Do you check her phone?
Is she to blame for how you feel, like when you get angry or upset?
Do you expect her to have sex when you want to, even if she is ill or asleep, or unwilling?
Do you say nasty things to her?
Do you think women and men are different and should behave differently?
Can your partner go out with who she likes when she likes?
Do you stop her from making her own decisions?
Do you hit or assault her?
Do you have control of her money?
Do you follow her or check on her movements

Domestic abuse roadmap for the abuser

Appendix 1.7

Abuse roadmap: this could happen if you don't stop

abuse
- She wants to leave
- depression, anger, trauma, alcohol
- friends, neighbours, family all know you can't cope

police
- police calls at your home and work
- removed from your home by force and not allowed to return
- police arrest and you go into custody
- police charge you with criminal offences

courts
- you are convicted – you have a rocord for violence against a woman
- you are punished – you may end up in prison
- you may lose your job and any chance of getting another
- you will lose the respect of people who know you

future
- you will lose everythink – you could lose your home, your job, your children, your freedon
- you will be labelled an abuser
- you could kill someone – this is a realistic possibility

Domestic abuse is not acceptable, you must stop now

Abuse is not just violence, abuse is about control. If you feel you need help to deal with depression, anger, alcohol or substance abuse, or other issues affecting your behaviour, you might want to consider getting some help before things get worse. There is information on this card to help you do this.

If you are abusive the police will get involved, as society does not accept this kind of behaviour.

There are many offences you could be convicted of: assault, threats to kill, harassment and stalking, witness intimidation, criminal damage, theft, and many more.

Stop and think.

THE POLICE WILL PROSECUTE YOU

Abuse will escalate and you will lose everything if you don't stop

Get help

Numbers....

Appendix 1.8

Stalking:

1. Is the abuser causing alarm, distress or a threat of violence?
2. Is the abuser making unwanted contact or attempting to?
3. Is the abuser publishing statements or material about the victim?
4. Is the abuser following the victim?
5. Is the abuser watching or spying on the victim?
6. Is the abuser interfering with property belonging to the victim?
7. Has the abuser attempted to gain entry/gained entry to the victim's property?
8. Has the victim changed their daily or other routine because of the harassment?

Consider context:

Is this incident part of ongoing behaviour?
Is it intended to instil fear?
Is it linked to control?
Pence and Sadusky (2009)
Stalking by a former or current partner is dangerous and should be taken seriously.

Notes

5 Police and Paramedics: Policy and Practice

1. *The Right to be Safe* (2010) www.cymru.gov.uk
2. *Together We Can End Violence Against Women and Girls: A Strategy* (2009) www.crimereduction.homeoffice.gov.uk/DA/DA01.htm
3. National Center for Injury Prevention and Control (2003) *Costs of Intimate Partner Violence Against Women in the United States*. Atlanta (GA): Centers for Disease Control and Prevention
4. American College of Emergency Physicians (2012) http://www.acep.org/Content.aspx?id=29186
5. *Policy and Guidance on Patients and Service Users Who Are Experiencing Domestic Abuse* V 2.2 (2010). Welsh Ambulance Services NHS Trust
6. *The Violence Against Women and Domestic Abuse Implementation Plan* (2010–2013) www.cymru.gov.uk
7. *Domestic Violence: A Resource Manual for Health Care Professionals in Wales* (2001), The National Assembly for Wales. www.wales.gov.uk/domesticviolence
8. Domestic violence and violence against women and children strategy and action plan 2010–2013
9. Tackling the Health Aspects of Violence Against Women and Children Stakeholder engagement report (2010)
10. Working Together for Success 2011–2016. Welsh Ambulance Services NHS Trust 2011.
11. Central and North West London (2007–2010) Domestic Abuse & Routine Enquiry Policy
12. Working Together for Success 2011–2016. Welsh Ambulance Services NHS Trust 2011.
13. Welsh Ambulance Services NHS Trust, HITS pocket aide memoire (2012)
14. Snapshot Clinical Audit of the Routine Enquiry into Domestic Abuse, using the HITS (DA1) Screening Tool (2011)
15. Griffiths, T. and Hinton, C. (2011) Snapshot Clinical Audit of the Routine Enquiry into Domestic Abuse, using the HITS (DA1) Screening Tool
16. Domestic Abuse : A Resource Manual for Health Care Professionals in Wales
17. Hyperlink to this advert: © 2012 Guardian News and Media Limited http://gu.com/p/5fyt

References

ABC (2010) Cada dos dias una mujer muere a manos de su parejer *ABC.es* Tuesday 13 April 2010, http://tinyurl.com/y3awdfl
Adams, D. (2007) *Why Do They Kill? Men Who Murder Their Intimate Partners* Nashville: Vanderbilt University Press
Allen, L. (2003) Girls Want Sex, Boys Want Love: Resisting Dominant Discourses of (Hetero) Sexuality *Sexualities* 6 (2): 215–236
Armour, M. (2002) Journey of Family Members of Homicide Victims: A Qualitative Study of their Posthomicide Experience *American Journal of Orthopsychiatry* 72 (3): 372–382
Baird, K., Salmon, D. and White, P. (2013) A Five Year Follow Up Study of the Bristol Pregnancy Domestic Violence Programme to Promote Routine Enquiry *Midwifery* 29: 1003–1010
BBC (2013) Emily Longley Murder: Elliott Turner Loses Appeal, BBC Online News 24 April 2013, http://www.bbc.co.uk/news/uk-england-dorset–22278528
BBC (2012) Raoul Moat Victim PC David Rathband Found Dead at Home, BBC Online News 1 January 2012, http://www.bbc.co.uk/news/uk-england-tyne-17216389
Benson, O. and Stangroom, J. (2009) *Does God Hate Women?* London: Continuum International Publishing
Berns, N. (2004) *Framing the Victim: Domestic Violence, Media and Social Problems* New York: Aldine De Gruyter
Black, B.M., Weisz, A.N. and Bennett, L. (2010) Graduating Social Work Students Perspectives on Domestic Violence *Affilia* 25 (2): 173–184
Bostrom, S.P. (2010) A Survivor's Point of View, Fatality Review Bulletin Summer, National Domestic Violence Fatality Review Initiative, http://www.ndvfri.org/newsletters/NDVFRI_Newsletter_2010Summer.pdf
Bradbury-Jones, C. and Taylor, J. (2013) Establishing a Domestic Abuse Care Pathway: Guidance for Practice *Nursing Standard* 27 (27): 42–47
Brown, J., James, K. and Taylor, A. (2010) Caught in the Rejection-Abuse Cycle: Are We Really Treating Perpetrators of Domestic Abuse Effectively? *Journal of Family Therapy* 32: 280–307
Brownmiller, S. (2000) *Against Our Will: Men Women and Rape* New York: Ballantine
CAADA (2014) Family Intervention Projects: Domestic Abuse Toolkit, http://www.caada.org.uk/marac/Toolkit-FIP-Feb-2012.pdf, accessed 10 May 2014
Cameron, D. House of Commons Liaison Committee, Oral evidence from the Prime Minister, 11 December 2012, HC 484-ii&iii, 2012–2013, Q112, http://www.publications.parliament.uk/pa/cm201213/cmselect/cmliaisn/484/484iI_iii.pdf, accessed 7 August 2013
Cammiss, S. (2006) The Management of Domestic Violence cases in Mode of Trial Hearing. Prosecutorial Control and Marginalising Victims *British Journal of Criminology* 46 (4): 704–718
Campbell, J. (2014) Personal Communication with Frank Mullane, July 2014

Campbell, J.C., Glass, N., Sharps, P.W., Laughon, K. and Bloom, T. (2007) Intimate Partner Homicide: Review and Implications of Research and Policy *Trauma Violence Abuse* 8: 246

Carabine, J. (2001) Unmarried Motherhood 1830–1990 A genealogical Analysis in *Discourse as Data* Wetherall, M., Taylor, S. and Yates, S.J. (eds) London: Sage

Caroline N. (2008) (6th edition) *Emergency Care in the Streets* London, Jones & Bartlett, ch 43: 10.

Casey, L. (2011) Review into the Needs of Families Bereaved by Homicide, http://www.justice.gov.uk/downloads/news/press-releases/victims-com/review-needs-of-families-bereaved-by-homicide.pdf

Chang, A. (2010) Honour Killings Confound Haryana India Realtime *The Wall Street Journal* 16 April 2010, http://tinyurl.com/y55lh59

Chanmugam, A. (2014) Social Work Expertise and Domestic Violence Fatality Review Teams *Social Work* 59 (1): 73–79

Christie, N. (1986) The Ideal Victim *From Crime Policy to Victim Policy: Reorienting the Justice System* Fattah, E. (ed.) London: Macmillan, 18

Cohen, S. (2002) *Folk Devils and Moral Panics* London: Routledge

Cooper, Y. (2013) Missed Calls for Help the Scandal of Domestic Violence *The Guardian* 5 February 2013

Dawson, M. (2003) The Cost of 'Lost' Intimacy: The Effect of Relationship State on Criminal Justice Decision Making *The British Journal of Criminology* 43 (4): 689–709

Dobash, R.E. and Dobash, R.P. (2002) (4th edition) *Women, Violence and Social Change* London: Routledge

Dodd, V. (2013) Mick Philpott Jailed for Life over Derby House Fire Which Killed Six Children *The Guardian*, http://www.theguardian.com/uk/2013/apr/04/mick-philpott-jailed-derby-fire

Douglas, H. and Walsh, T. (2010) Mothers, Domestic Violence and Child Protection *Violence Against Women* 1 (6): 489–509

Echeburua, E. and Fernandez-Montalvo, J. (2007) Male Batterers with and without Psychopathy: An exploratory study in Spanish Prisons *International Journal of Offender Therapy and Comparative Criminology* 51 (3): 254–263

Felder, R. and Victor, B. (1997) *Getting Away with Murder: Weapons for the War against Domestic Violence*. New York: Touchstone

Felson, M. and Clarke, R.V. (1998) *Opportunity Makes the Thief: Practical Theory for Crime Prevention* London: Home Office, http://webarchive.nationalarchives.gov.uk/20110218135832/rds.homeoffice.gov.uk/rds/prgpdfs/fprs98.pdf

Flood, M. (2009) Violence against Women and Men in Australia. What the Personal Safety Survey Can and Can't Tell Us about Domestic Violence *XY online*, http://www.xyonline.net/content/violence-against-women-and-men-australia-what-personal-safety-survey-can-and-cant-tell-us-ab

Fogarty, K., Augoustinos, M. and Kettler, L. (2013) Re-Thinking Rapport through the Lens of Progressivity in Investigative Interviews into Child Sexual Abuse *Discourse Studies* 15 (4): 395–420

Foucault, M. (1978) *The History of Sexuality 1: An Introduction* trans Robert Hurley Hammondsworth: Penguin

Foucault, M. (1972) *The Archaeology of Knowledge and the Discourse on Language* trans. Sheridan Smith, A.M. New York: Pantheon

Gadd, D. (2012) Domestic Abuse Prevention after Raoul Moat *Critical Social Policy* 32 (4): 495–516

Gondolf, E.W. (2010) The Contributions of Ellen Pence to Batterer Programming *Violence Against Women* 16 (9): 992–1006

Gover, A.R., Dagmar, P.P. and Dodge, M. (2011) Law Enforcement Officers Attitudes about Domestic Violence *Violence Against Women* 17 (5): 619–636

Hall, M. (2009) Prosecuting Domestic Violence: New Solutions to Old Problems? *International Review of Victimology* 1(5): 255–276

Harne, L. and Radford, J. (2008) *Tackling Domestic Violence; Theories, Policies and Practice* Berkshire: Open University Press

Hester, M. (2013a) Thames Valley Police *Domestic Abuse Master Class* Oxford October 2013

Hester, M. (2013b) Who Does What to Whom? Gender and Domestic Violence Perpetrators in English Police Records *European Journal of Criminology* 10 (5): 623–667

Hester, M. (2009) *Who Does What to Whom? Gender and Domestic Violence Perpetrators* University of Bristol and Northern Rock Foundation, Bristol

Hester M. and Westmarland N. (2006) *Service Provision for Perpetrators of Domestic Violence* Bristol: University of Bristol

HMIC (2014) Everyone's Business: Improving the Police Response to Domestic Abuse HMIC

Home Office (2013) Multi-Agency Statutory Guidance for the Conduct of Domestic Homicide Reviews. Revised – Applicable to All Notifications Made from and Including 1 August 2013, https://www.gov.uk/government/uploads/system/uploads/attachment_data/file/209020/DHR_Guidance_refresh_HO_final_WEB.pdf

Home Office (2012) *New Definition of Domestic Violence,* http://www.homeoffice.gov.uk/media-centre/news/domestic-violence-definition

House of Commons (2014) Adjournment Debate, HC Deb 4 March 2014, Vol 576 cc272–280WH

Hoyle, C. and Palmer, N. (2014) Family Justice Centres: A Model for Empowerment *International Review of Victimology* 20: 191

Huss, M. (2009) *Violence and Forensic Psychology* Chichester: Wiley

Jaffe, P.G., Campbell, M., Hamilton, L.H.A. and Juodis, M. (2012) Children in Danger of Domestic Homicide *Child Abuse and Neglect* 36 (2012): 71–74

Jaffe, P.G., Dawson, M. and Campbell, M. (2013) Developing a National Collaborative Approach to Prevent Domestic Homicides: Domestic Homicide Review Committees *Canadian Journal of Criminology and Criminal Justice* January 2013

Jewell, L.M. and Wormith, S.J. (2010) Variables Associated with Attrition From Domestic Violence Treatment Programmes Targeting Male Batterers: A Meta Analysis *Criminal Justice and Behavior* 3 (7): 1086–1114

Juodis, M., Starzomski, A., Porter, S. and Woodworth, M. (2014) A Comparison of Domestic and Non-Domestic Homicides: Further Evidence for Distinct Dynamics and Heterogeneity of Domestic Homicide Perpetrators. *Journal of Family Violence* 29 (3): 299–313

Kelly, L., Lovett, J. and Regan, L. (2005) *A Gap or a Chasm? Attrition in Reported Rape Cases.* Home Office Research Study 293. London: HMSO

Kilpatrick, D.G., Amick, A. and resnick, H.S. (1990) The Impact of Homicide on Surviving Family Members US Dept of Justice, https://www.ncjrs.gov/pdffiles1/Digitization/130823NCJRS.pdf

Kimmel, M. (2008) 'Gender Symmetry' in Domestic Violence: A Falsely Framed Issue in *Domestic Violence. a Multi-Professional Approach for Healthcare Practitioners* Keeling, J. and Mason, T. (eds) Berkshire: Open University Press

Kirby, S., Francis, B. and O'Flaherty, R. (2014) Can the FIFA World Cup Football (Soccer) Tournament be Associated with an Increase in Domestic Abuse? *Journal of Research in Crime and Delinquency* 51: 259

Lees, S. (1997) *Ruling Passions. Sexual Violence, Reputation and the Law* Buckingham: Open University Press

Liem, M. and Roberts, D.W. (2009) Intimate Partner Homicide by Presence or Absence of a Self-Destructive Act *Homicide Studies* 13: 399

Lindhorst, T., Meyers, M. and Casey, E. (2008) Screeing for Domestic Violence in Public Welfare Offices: An Analysis of Case Manager and Client Interactions *Violence Against Women* 14: 5–29

Lonsway, K.A. (2006) Domestic Violence: Prevalence and Specific Provisions within Large Police Agencies *Police Quarterly* 9 (4): 397–422

Macy, R.J., Giattina, M.C., Johns Montijo, N. and Ermentrout, D.M. (2010) Domestic Violence and Sexual assault Agency Directors Perspectives on Services that Help Survivors *Violence Against Women* 16: 1138–1162

Macy, R.J., Giattina, M.C., Parish, S.L. and Crosby, C. (2009) Domestic Violence and Sexual assault Services: Historical Concerns and Contemporary Challenges *Journal of Interpersonal Violence* 25: 3–34

Mahapatro, M., Gupta, R.N., Gupta, V. and Kundu, A.S. (2011) Domestic Violence During Pregnancy in India *Journal of Interpersonal Violence* 26 (15): 2973–2990

Matczak, A. et al. (2011) *Review of Domestic Violence policies in England and Wales* London: Kingston

Matthews, S., Abrahams, N., Martin, L., Vetten, L., van der Merwe, L. and Jewkes, R. (2004) Every Six Hours a Woman Is Killed by Her Intimate Partner *A National Study of Female Homicide in South Africa*. Gender and Health Research Group, Medical Research Council, Tygerberg: 2

McGarry, J. (2013) Developing a New Post for Nurses to Identify Cases of Domestic Abuse *Emergency Nurse* June 21: 3

Messent, M. (2014) Our 'Holy Cows' Are Own Worst Enemies Birmingham Mail 4 April, http://www.birminghammail.co.uk/news/news-opinion/maureen-messent-domestic-abuse-against-6918862#.U2fEL2y9qgU.twitter

Messing, J.T. and Heeren, J.W. (2009) Gendered Justice: Domestic Homicide and the Death Penalty *Feminist Criminology* 4: 170

Ministry of Justice (2012) Getting It Right for Victims and Witnesses: The Government Response, https://consult.justice.gov.uk/digital-communications/victims-witnesses

Monckton Smith, J. (2012) *Murder, Gender and the Media: Narratives of Dangerous Love* Hampshire: Palgrave Macmillan

Monckton Smith, J. (2011) *An Evaluation of the Phoenix Programme* Blaenau Gwent Domestic Abuse Services

Monckton Smith, J. (2010) *Relating Rape and Murder: Narratives of sex, Death and Gender* Hampshire: Palgrave Macmillan

Monckton Smith, J., Adams,T., Hart, A. and Webb, J. (2013) *Introducing Forensic and Criminal Investigation* London: Sage

Morris, K., Brandon, M. and Tudor, P. (2012) 'a Study of Family Involvement in Case Reviews. Messages for Policy and Practice': British Association for the Study and Prevention of Child Abuse and Neglect (BASPCAN), http://www.baspcan.org.uk/report.php

Muller, R. (2014) Eder Abuse: A Growing Problem in an Aging Population *Psychology Today* published online January 2014, http://www.psychologytoday.com/blog/talking-about-trauma/201401/elder-abuse-growing-problem-in-aging-population

Munby, J. (2008) England and Wales High Court (Family Division) Decisions *Re N [2008] EWHC 2042* National Domestic Violence Fatality Review Initiative http://ndvfri.org/

National Stalking Helpline (2014) http://www.stalkinghelpline.org/

Nelson, E.L. (2014) If You Want to Convict a Domestic Violence Batterer List Multiple Charges in the Police Report *Sage Open* January 4 (1)

NSPCC (2014) National Society for the Prevention of Cruelty to Children (2011) Childline Case Notes, http://www.nspcc.org.uk/Inform/publications/casenotes/childline_casenotes_wda47964.html, accessed 10 May 2014

Othman, S., Goddard, C. and Piterman, L. (2014) Victims Barriers to Discussing Domestic Violence in Cinical Consultations: A Qualitative Enquiry *Journal of Interpersonal Violence* 29: (8) : 1497–1513

Overlien, C. (2010) Children Exposed to Domestic Violence. Conclusions From the Literature and Challenges Ahead *Journal of Social Work* 10 (1): 80–97

Pain, R. (2014) Everyday Terrorism. Connecting Domestic Violence and Global Terrorism *Progress in Human Geography* 38 (4): 531–550

Pain, R. (2013) *Everyday Terrorism: How Fear Works in Domestic Abuse*, https://www.dur.ac.uk/resources/geography/downloads/EverydayTerrorism.pdf

Passmore, D. and Weston, P. (2011) http://www.couriermail.com.au/news/queensland/new-investigative-unit-will-reopen-cases-after-coroner-fears-hidden-domestic-violence-death-toll/story-e6freoof-1226060294225

Pence, E., and Paymar, M. (1993) *Education Groups for Men Who Batter: The Duluth Model* New York: Springer

Pence, E. and Sadusky, J. (2009) *Engage to Protect: Foundations for Supervised Visitation and Exchange. Recognising and Understanding Battering*, http://www.praxisinternational.org/files/praxis/files/Visitation%20TA/EngagetoProtectRecognizingandUnderstandingBatteringPaper.pdf

Peters, J. (2008) Domestic Violence Myths in *Domestic Violence. a Multi-Professional Approach for Healthcare Professionals* Keeling, J. and Mason, T. (eds) Berkshire: McGraw Hill Open University Press

Polk, K. (1994) *When Men Kill. Scenarios of Masculine Violence* Cambridge: Cambridge University Press

Practical Law (2008) http://uk.practicallaw.com/7–383–1384?service=dispute

Raj, A. and Silverman, J.G. (2007) Domestic Violence Help Seeking Behaviours of South Asian Battered Women Residing in the United States *International Review of Victimology* 14: 143–171

Reckdenwald, A. and Palmer, K.F. (2000) Understanding the Change in Male and Female Intimate Partner Homicide Over Time: A Policy and Theory Relevant Investigation *Feminist Criminology* 7: 167

Richards, L. (2010) *DASH (2009) Frequently Asked Questions* available at: http://tinyurl.com/3yr8z6y

Richards, L. (2006) Homicide Prevention: The Findings from the Multi-Agency Domestic Homicide Reviews *Journal of Homicide and Major Incident Investigation* 2 (2): Autumn

Roberts, R. (2013) Is Criminal Justice a Form of Violence against Women? Centre for Crime and Justice Studies, http://www.crimeandjustice.org.uk/resources/criminal-justice-form-violence-against-women

Rock, P. (1998) *After Homicide: Practical and Political Responses to Bereavement.* Oxford: Clarendon Press

Roehl, J., O'sullivan, C., Webster, D. and Campbell, J. (2005) Intimate Partner Violence Risk Assessment Validation Risk Study: Final Report, https://www.ncjrs.gov/pdffiles1/nij/grants/209731.pdf

Schwartz, A. (2010) Strangulation and Domestic Violence Important Changes in New York Criminal and Domestic Violence Law Empire Justice Centre, http://www.empirejustice.org/issue-areas/domestic-violence/case-laws-statues/criminal/strangulation-and-domestic.html

Scott, K. (2004) Predictors of Change Among Male Batterers. Application of Theories and Review of Empirical Findings *Trauma Violence Abuse* 5 (3): 260–284

Sloan-Lynch, J. (2012) Domestic Abuse as Terrorism *Hypatia* 27 (4): 774–790

Smart, C. (1989) *Feminism and the Power of Law* London: Routledge

Smith, E. (2011) A Qualitative Review of Perception of Change for Male Perpetrators of Domestic Abuse Following Abuser Schema Therapy *Counselling and Psychotherapy Research* June 11 (2): 156–164

Snider, C., Webster, D., O'Sullivan, C. and Campbell, J. (2009) Intimate Partner Violence Development of a Brief Risk Assessment for the Emergency Department *Academic Emergency Medicine* 16 (11): 1208–1216

Sohal, A., Feder, G. and Johnson, M. (2012) Domestic Violence and Abuse *Innovait* 5: 12

Sokoloff, N. and Dupont, I. (2005) Domestic Violence at the Intersections of Race, Class and Gender: Challenges and Contributions to Understanding Violence Against Marginalized Women in Diverse Communities *Violence Against Women* 11: 38–64

Stark, E. (2013) *Domestic Abuse Master Class* Thames Valley Police Oxford October 2013

Stark, E. (2012) The Dangers of Dangerousness Assessment *Domestic Violence Report* 17 (5): 65–80

Stark, E. (2009) Rethinking Coercive Control *Violence Against Women* 15 (12): 1509–1525

Stark, E. (2007) *Coercive Control: The Entrapment of Women in Everyday Life* Oxford: Oxford University Press

Starzomski, A. and Nussbaum, D. (2000) The Self and the Psychology of Domestic Homicide – Suicide *International Journal of Offender Therapy and Comparative Criminology* 44: 468

Stewart, D.E., MacMillan, H. and Wathen, N. (2012) Intimate Partner Violence Canadian Psychiatric Association Position Paper *Canadian Journal of Psychiatry* 58: 6

Sullivan Wilson, J. and Websdale, N. (2006) Domestic Violence Fatality Review Teams: An Interprofessional Model to Reduce Deaths *Journal of Interprofessional Care* October 20 (5): 535–544

Sweetnam, S. (2013) Where Do You Think Domestic Abuse Hurts Most? *Violence Against Women* 19 (1): 133–138

Swogger, M.T., Walsh, Z. and Kosson, D.S. (2007) Domestic Violence and Psychopathic Traits: Distinguishing the Antisocial Batterer from other Antisocial Offenders *Aggressive Behaviour* 33: 1–8

Szilassy, E., Carperneter, J., Patsios, D. and Hackett, S. (2014) Outcomes of Interprofessional Training in Domestic Violence and Child Protection *Violence Against Women* 19 (11): 1370–1383

Taket, A. et al. (2003) Routinely Asking Women About Domestic Violence in Health Settings *British Medical Journal* 327: 673–676

Tanenbaum, L. (2007) *Slut! Growing Up Female with a Bad Reputation* New York: Seven Stories Press

Thornton, P. Chief Coroner (2013) Implementation of Relevant Parts of Coroners and Justice Act 2009, News Release 25 July 2013, http://www.judiciary.gov.uk/media/media-releases/2013/ChiefCoronerImplementationOfRelevantPartsOfCoronersAndJusticeAct2009

Thorp, D. (1992) The Social Construction of Homosexuality *Phoenix* 46 (1): 54–65, http://www.fordham.edu/halsall/med/thorp.asp

Thurston, W., Tutty, L.M., Eisener, A.C., Lalonde, L., Belenky, C. and Osborne, B. (2009) Implementation of Universal Screening for Domestic Violence in an Emergency Care Community Health Centre *Health Promotion Practice* 10 (4): 517–526

Trevillion, K., Agnew-Davies, R. and Howard, L. (2013) Healthcare Professionals Response to Domestic Violence *Primary Health Care* 23 (9): 34–42

Van Wijk, J. (2013) Who Is the 'Little Old Lady' of International Crimes? Nils Christie's Concept of the Ideal Victim Reinterpreted *International Review of Victimology* 19: 159

Van Wormer, K. and Roberts, A. (2009) *Death by Domestic Violence Preventing the Murders and Murder Suicides* Westport USA: Praeger

Van Wormer, K. and Roberts, A. (2008) Partner Homicide Including Murder-Suicide: Gender Differences in *Domestic Violence. A Multi-Professional Approach for Healthcare Professionals* Keeling, J. and Mason, T. (eds) Berkshire: McGraw Hill Open University Press

Volochinsky, B.P. (2012) Obtaining Justice for Victims of Strangulation in Domestic Violence: Evidence Based Prosecution and Strangulation-Specific Training *Student Pulse* 4 (10): 1–4, http://www.studentpulse.com/articles/706/obtaining-justice-for-victims-of-strangulation-in-domestic-violence-evidence-based-prosecution-and-strangulation-specific-training

VPC (2005) *When Men Murder Women: An Analysis of 2003 Homicide Data* Violence Policy Center, Washington, DC, http://www.vpc.org/studies/wmmw2005.pdf

Walby, S. (2004) *The Cost of Domestic Violence* Women and Equality Unit, http://www.lancs.ac.uk/fass/sociology/papers/walby-costdomesticviolence.pdf

Walker, M., McGlade M. and Gamble J. (2008) A Domestic Homicide Review into the Deaths of Julia and William Pemberton; a Report for West Berkshire Safer Communities Partnership, West Berkshire Council, http://www.westberks.gov.uk/index.aspx?articleid=16085

Walklate, S. (2008) What Is to Be Done about Violence against Women? *British Journal of Criminology* 48(1): 39–54

Walklate, S. and Mythen, G. (2011) Beyond Risk Theory *Criminology & Criminal Justice* 11(2): 99–113

Websdale, N. (2010) *Familicidal Hearts* Oxford: Oxford University Press
Websdale, N. (2001) Domestic Violence Fatality Reviews: Implications for Law Enforcement *The Police Chief* July
Websdale, N. (1999) *Understanding Domestic Homicide* Boston: Northeastern University Press
Weller, M., Hope, L. and Sheridan, L. (2013) Police and public Perceptions of Stalking: The Role of Prior Victim Offender Relationship *Journal of Interpersonal Violence* 28(2): 320–339
Wilson, D. (2009) Comment is Free, *The Guardian* 5 November 2009, http://bit.ly/16vGgXQ
Women's Aid (2014) What Is the Cost of Domestic Violence, http://www.womensaid.org.uk/domestic-violencearticles.asp?section=00010001002200410001&itemid=1272, accessed 21 April 2014
Woodworth, M., Hancock, J., Porter, s., Hare, R., Logan, M., O'Toole, M.E. and Smith, S. (2012) The Language of Psychopaths. New Findings and Implications for Law Enforcement *FBI Law Enforcement Bulletin*, http://www.fbi.gov/stats-services/publications/law-enforcement-bulletin/july-2012/the-language-of-psychopaths

Index

Printed and bound by CPI Group (UK) Ltd, Croydon, CR0 4YY